Mathcounts Speed and Accuracy Practice Tests

http://www.mymathcounts.com/index.php

About the book:

The book contains ten tests that can be used to train students' speed and accuracy during Mathcounts competitions at school, chapter, state, and national levels. Each test has two parts. Part I trains students calculation speed with number sense. Part II trains students reading and problem solving skills. Each problem in Part II has the detained solutions.

Copyright © 2016, 2014 by mymathcounts.com

All rights reserved. Printed in the United States of America

Reproduction of any portion of this book without the written permission of the authors is strictly prohibited, except as may be expressly permitted by the U.S. Copyright Act.

ISBN-13: 978-1499276893
ISBN-10: 1499276893

Please contact mymathcounts@gmail.com for suggestions, corrections, or clarifications.

Table of Contents

1. Test 1   1

2. Test 2   19

3. Test 3   35

4. Test 4   53

5. Test 5   71

6. Test 6   90

7. Test 7   107

8. Test 8   126

9. Test 9   143

10. Test 10   161

This page is intentionally left blank.

MATHCOUNTS

■ **Speed and Accuracy Practice Test 1**■

Name

Date

DO NOT BEGIN UNTIL YOU ARE INSTRUCTED TO DO SO.
The test consists of two parts, with each part 40 problems. You will have 15 minutes to complete the part 1 and 25 minutes to complete the part 2. You are not allowed to use calculators, books, or any other aids during this round. Calculations may be done on scratch paper. All answers must be complete, legible, and simplified to lowest terms. Record only final answers. Do each problem as quick as you can. If you finish one problem, go to the next. Do not spend any time to check your answers.

	Total Correct	Scorer's Initials
Part I		
Part II		

©www.mymathcounts.com

Mathcounts Speed and Accuracy Practice Test 1

Part I Problems 1–40

Mathcounts Speed and Accuracy Practice Tests — Test 1

1. 50% of 130 is

2. $(16 \times 100) + (13 \times 10) + (7 \times 1) =$

3. $31 + 57 + 69 =$

4. $3521 \div 7 =$

5. $\dfrac{1}{3} - \dfrac{1}{4} =$

6. $45 \div 2\dfrac{1}{2} =$

7. Find the sum:
$\dfrac{1}{1\times 2} + \dfrac{1}{2\times 3} + \dfrac{1}{3\times 4} + \dfrac{1}{4\times 5}$.

8. 25 quarters + 10 dimes = $ —

9. $7441 \div 7$ has a remainder of ——

10. $2214 \div 18$ has a remainder of ——

11. Simplify: $\dfrac{1}{1+\dfrac{1}{1+\dfrac{1}{1}}}$. Express your answer as a common fraction.

12. $5.6 \times 16.5 \div 0.7 \div 1.1 =$

13. $13 \times 14 + 7 \times 14 =$

14. The perimeter of a square with area 144 is —

15. $37^2 =$

16. Express as a decimal: 1001×3.63

17. 2.5 square meters = —— square decimeters

18. $18^2 - 17^2 =$

19. Write base 9 number 27_9 in base 10.

20. Express as a common fraction: $\dfrac{3\dfrac{1}{0.2}}{0.75}$

21. Simplify: $20\% \cdot (100 + 200 + 300 + 400)$.

22. Simplify: $37\dfrac{1}{2}\% \times \dfrac{600}{75} \times 8\dfrac{1}{3}\%$

23. Express $11\frac{1}{9}\%$ as a common fraction.

24. 19 is 5% of —

25. Calculate: $2 \div 0.125$

26. $\sqrt{1681} =$

27. The next term in the sequence 3, 6, 4, 7, 5, … is —

28. $0.\overline{12} = $ —— fraction

29. Express $12\frac{1}{5} \times 3\frac{1}{5}$ as a mixed number.

30. Write the fraction equivalent to $62\frac{1}{2}\%$.

31. If the length and width of a rectangle are 8 and 15, then the diagonal is

32. Find the slope of the line $x - 3y = 9$.

33. $\sqrt{99}$ simplified is =

34. $6! \div 5! =$

35. Express as a decimal: $3\frac{2}{10} \times 4\frac{7}{10}$

36. The number of combinations of 6 items taken 3 at a time is

37. How many of the first 11 positive integers have reciprocals that are repeating decimals?

38. The surface area of a sphere with diameter 10 is — .

39. Express $\sqrt{5\frac{19}{25}}$ as a common fraction.

40. If the circumference of a circle is 8π, what is its area?

Mathcounts Speed and Accuracy Practice Test 1

Part II Problems 41–80

Mathcounts Speed and Accuracy Practice Tests — Test 1

41. If 24 students in a class of 30 students were present, what percent of the students were absent?

42. A line with slope 2/3 contains the point P(1, –2). What is the x-intercept of the line?

43. The arithmetic mean of seven numbers is 23. What is their sum?

44. The lengths of the sides of a triangle are x, 19 and 31 units. How many integer values of x are possible?

45. A customer was one day late paying a credit card bill in the amount of $500 and was charged a 2.5% late fee. What was the amount, in dollars, of the late fee? Express your answer as a decimal to the nearest hundredth.

46. What common fraction with a value between 0.8 and 0.9 inclusive has the smallest denominator?

47. A bug moves 8 inch up and then 15 inches to the right on a piece of paper. How many inches is the bug from its original position?

48. For how many integer values of n does $n^2 = \sqrt{|n|}$?

49. What is the number of square inches in the area of an equilateral triangle with a side length of 8 inches? Express your answer in simplest radical form.

50. The five-digit number 34,6n8 is divisible by 9. What is the value of the digit n?

51. What is the greatest positive three-digit integer divisible by both 7 and 9?

Mathcounts Speed and Accuracy Practice Tests — Test 1

52. How many ways can $13 be made using only quarters and/or dimes?

53. The rectangular pool X is four times as long and twice as wide as the rectangular pool Y. The depths of both pools are the same. The volume of the pool X is how many times as great as the volume of the pool Y?

54. A number is 36 less than its additive inverse. What is the number?

55. The arithmetic mean of 5, 5 and x is 5.5. What is the value of x? Express your answer as a decimal to the nearest tenth.

56. What is the largest three-digit multiple of 3 whose digits sum is 24?

57. The cost of 10 pencils is $0.94. At the same rate, what is the cost, in dollars, of 35 pencils? Express your answer as a decimal to the nearest hundredth.

58. Find the number of positive integer values of n such that $3n$ is a factor of $6!$?

59. In how many different ways can 12 dimes be divided into three piles with at least one dime in each pile?

60. The ratio of the number of junior high students to the number of senior high students in a school is 6 to 11. If there are 100 more senior high students than junior high students, how many junior high students are there?

61. What is the number of square centimeters in the area of one 30° sector of a circle of radius 24 centimeters? Express your answer in terms of π.

62. In a barn with horses and chickens, the number of legs was 18 more than twice the number of heads. How many horses were in the barn?

Mathcounts Speed and Accuracy Practice Tests   Test 1

63. How many meters longer is the circumference of a circle with radius 100 meters than the circumference of a circle with radius 50 meters? Express your answer in terms of π.

64. By what common fraction does $0.\overline{21}$ exceed 0.21?

65. If $n = 4^2$, then what is the value of n^2?

66. From the twelve members of the math club, a president, a vice president and a treasurer are selected. In how many different ways can three distinct members be chosen to fill the positions?

67. Using an exercise bike, Chip burns 270 calories during 18 minutes of exercise. At this rate, what is the total number of calories Chip burns during 30 minutes of exercise on the bike?

68. Alicia is 160 centimeters tall. On a sunny day, she casts a 220-centimeter shadow at the same time that a flagpole casts a 33-meter shadow. How many meters tall is the flagpole?

69. Two angles of a triangle have a ratio of 5 to 7. The third angle has a measure of 72 degrees. What is the measure in degrees of the largest angle in the triangle?

70. The cost to send a person to Mars is estimated to be $45 billion. If the cost is equally shared by 5% of the 250 million U.S. citizens, how many dollars are in each citizen's share?

71. What is the probability that four tosses of a fair coin result in exactly two heads and two tails? Express your answer as a common fraction.

72. What is the probability that if you roll two fair, standard six sided dice, the difference between the two numbers rolled will be 1? Express your answer as a common fraction.

Mathcounts Speed and Accuracy Practice Tests   **Test 1**

73. How many more sides does an octagonal prism have than an octagonal pyramid?

74. What is the arithmetic mean of all positive three-digit multiples of 6?

75. A cone and a cylinder have the same height and a base with the same diameter. What is the ratio of the volume of the cone to the volume of the cylinder? Express your answer as a common fraction.

76. Maria designs a six-pointed star by drawing an equilateral triangle on each side of a regular hexagon as shown in the diagram. The length of each side of the hexagon is 2 cm. What is the number of square centimeters in the area of Maria's star? Express your answer in simplest radical form.

77. If x is 60% of y, what percent of $3y$ is $4x$?

78. There are 52 students in a class. 30 of them can swim. 35 can ride bicycle. 42 can play table tennis. At least how many students can do all three sports?

79. A road construction unit is made up of a certain number of workers and a certain amount of equipment. Three units have paved 20 miles of a road in 10 days. How many additional units are needed if the remaining 50 miles of the road must be paved in 15 days?

80. How many ordered pairs of integer numbers (x, y) satisfy the equation $\dfrac{\frac{1}{x}+\frac{1}{y}}{1-\frac{1}{xy}}=\dfrac{1}{10}$?

Mathcounts Speed and Accuracy Practice Tests — Test 1

Answer Keys:

PART I

1. 65
2. 1737
3. 157
4. 503
5. $\frac{1}{12}$
6. 18
7. $\frac{4}{5}$
8. 7.25
9. 0
10. 0
11. $\frac{2}{3}$
12. 120.
13. 280
14. 48
15. 1369
16. 3633.63
17. 250
18. 35
19. 25_{10}
20. 99/10
21. 200.
22. 25
23. $\frac{1}{9}$
24. 380
25. 16.
26. 41
27. 8
28. $\frac{4}{33}$
29. $39\frac{1}{25}$
30. 5/8.
31. 17
32. $\frac{1}{3}$
33. $3\sqrt{11}$
34. 6
35. 15.04
36. 20
37. 5
38. 100π
39. $\frac{12}{5}$
40. 16π.

Mathcounts Speed and Accuracy Practice Tests — Test 1

PART II

41. 20%.

42. 4.

43. 161.

44. 37.

45. $12.50.

46. $\frac{4}{5}$.

47. 17.

48. 3.

49. $16\sqrt{3}$.

50. 6.

51. 945.

52. 61.

53. 8.

54. –18.

55. 6.5.

56. 996.

57. 3.29.

58. 8.

59. 12.

60. 120.

61. 48π.

62. 9.

63. 100π.

64. 7/3300.

65. 256.

66. 1320.

67. 450.

68. 24.

69. 72.

70. 3,600.

71. $\frac{3}{8}$.

72. 5/18.

73. 8.

74. 549.

75. 1/3.

76. $12\sqrt{3}$.

77. 80%.

78. 3.

79. 2.

80. 4 pairs.

Mathcounts Speed and Accuracy Practice Tests Test 1

Solutions to Part II:

41. Solution: 20%.

The number of student who were absent: 30 – 24 = 6.

6/ 30 = 0.2 = 20%.

42. Solution: 4.
The line can be described as $\frac{y+2}{x-1} = \frac{2}{3}$.

We obtain the x-intercept of the line by letting y = 0: $\frac{0+2}{x-1} = \frac{2}{3}$ $\Rightarrow$ x = 4.

43. Solution: 161.
The sum will be 7 × 23 = 161.

44. Solution: 37.
By the Triangle Inequality Theorem:
$\quad\quad$ 19 + 31 > x $\quad\Rightarrow\quad$ x < 50
$\quad\quad$ 19 + x > 31 $\quad\Rightarrow\quad$ x > 12
So we get 12 < x < 50.
The integer values are from 13 to 49. The answer is 49 – 13 + 1 = 37

45. Solution: $12.50.
$\frac{2.5}{100} \times 500 = 12.5$.

46. Solution: $\frac{4}{5}$.

We want the smallest denominator. We check
$\frac{3}{4}, \frac{4}{5}, \frac{5}{6}, \frac{6}{7}$. The answer is $\frac{4}{5}$.

47. Solution: 17.
By the Pythagorean Theorem, $\sqrt{8^2 + 15^2} = \sqrt{289} = 17$.

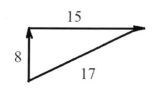

48. Solution: 3.

Mathcounts Speed and Accuracy Practice Tests   Test 1

$n^2 = \sqrt{|n|} \implies n^4 = |n|$ (1)

Case 1: $n^4 - n = 0 \implies n(n^3 - 1) = 0 \implies n = 0$ or $n = 1$.
Case 2: $n^4 + n = 0 \implies n(n^3 + 1) = 0 \implies n = 0$ or $n = -1$.
The answer is 3.

49. Solution: $16\sqrt{3}$.

The area of an equilateral triangle is: $A = \frac{\sqrt{3}}{4}a^2$. We know that $a = 8$.

So $A = \frac{\sqrt{3}}{4} \times 8^2 = 16\sqrt{3}$.

50. Solution: 6.
The sum of the digits must be divisible by 9.
$3 + 4 + 6 + n + 8 = 3 + n$ must be divisible by 9. So n is 6.

51. Solution: 945.
The number must be divisible by 63.
$999 = 15 \times 63 + 54$. So the number divisible by 63 is $999 - 54 = 945$.

52. Solution: 61.

$25q + 10d = 1500 \quad\implies\quad 5q + 2d = 300$.
The greatest value of q is $300/5 = 60$ and the smallest value of q is 0. The answer is 61.

53. Solution: 8.
$\dfrac{V_X}{V_Y} = \dfrac{4L \cdot 2W \cdot D}{L \cdot W \cdot D} = 8$.

54. Solution: -18.
$n = -n - 36 \quad\implies\quad 2n = -36 \quad\implies\quad n = -18$

55. Solution: 6.5.
$\dfrac{5 + 5 + x}{3} = 5.5 \quad\implies\quad 5 + 5 + x = 5.5 \times 3 \quad\implies\quad x = 16.5 - 10 = 6.5$

56. Solution: 996.

The greatest value of the 3-digit number divisible by 3 is 999. But the sum of the digits of 999 is not 24.

The greatest value of the 3-digit number with the digit sum of 24 is 996 and 996 is divisible by 3.

57. Solution: 3.29.
Let x be the cost.
$$\frac{10}{0.94} = \frac{35}{x} \quad \Rightarrow x = \$3.29.$$

58. Solution: 8.
$6! = 120 = 3(40) = 3(2^3 \times 5)$.
There are $4 \times 2 = 8$ factors of $(2^3 \times 5)$. So there are 8 values of n.
(1, 2, 4, 5, 8, 10, 20, 40).

59. Solution: 12.
Method 1:
$12 = 10 + 1 + 1 = 9 + 2 + 1 = 8 + 3 + 1 = 8 + 2 + 2 = 7 + 4 + 1 = 7 + 3 + 2 = 6 + 5 + 1 = 6 + 4 + 2 = 6 + 3 + 3 = 5 + 5 + 2 = 5 + 4 + 3 = 4 + 4 + 4$.

Method 2:
$$P(n,3) = \left\lfloor \frac{n^2}{12} \right\rfloor \quad \Rightarrow \quad P(12,3) = \left\lfloor \frac{12^2}{12} \right\rfloor = 12.$$

Method 3:
$P(n,k) = P(n-1, k-1) + P(n-k, k)$. $P(n,1) = P(n, n-1) = P(n,n) = 1$.
$P(12,3) = P(11,2) + P(9,3) = P(10,1) + P(9,2) + P(8,2) + P(6,3)$
$= 1 + P(8,1) + P(7,2) + P(7,1) + P(6,2) + P(5,2) + P(3,3)$
$= 1 + 1 + P(7,2) + 1 + P(6,2) + P(5,2) + 1$
$= 4 + P(7,2) + P(6,2) + P(5,2) = 4 + P(6,1) + P(5,2) + P(5,1) + P(4,2) + P(4,1) + P(2,2)$
$= 4 + 1 + P(5,2) + 1 + P(4,2) + 1 + 1 = 8 + P(5,2) + P(4,2)$
$= 8 + P(4,1) + P(3,2) + P(3,1) + P(2,2) = 8 + 1 + 1 + 1 + 1 = 12$.

60. Solution: 120.
$\dfrac{J}{S} = \dfrac{6}{11} \quad \Rightarrow \quad 11J = 6S \quad (1)$
$J + 100 = S \quad (2)$

Mathcounts Speed and Accuracy Practice Tests   Test 1

Substituting (2) into (1): $11J = 6(J+100) \implies 5J = 600 \implies J = 120$.

61. Solution: 48π.

Let the area be x. By proportion property: $\dfrac{360°}{\pi r^2} = \dfrac{30°}{x} \implies \dfrac{360°}{\pi \cdot 24^2} = \dfrac{30°}{x} \implies x = 48\pi$.

62. Solution: 9.
Let the number of horses be h and the number of chickens be c.
The number of legs will be $4h + 2c$.
The number of heads will be $h + c$.
We know that the number of legs was 18 more than twice the number of heads.
So $4h + 2c = 2(h + c) + 18 \implies 2h = 18 \implies h = 9$.

63. Solution: 100π.
$2\pi R - 2\pi r = 2\pi(R - r) = 2\pi \cdot 50 = 100\pi$.

64. Solution: 7/3300.
$0.\overline{21} - 0.21 = \dfrac{21}{99} - \dfrac{21}{100} = \dfrac{2100 - 2079}{9900} = \dfrac{21}{9900} = \dfrac{7}{3300}$.

65. Solution: 256.
$n^2 = (4^2)^2 = 16^2 = 256$.

66. Solution: 1320.
Method 1:
We use the permutation method: $P(12,3) = 12 \times 11 \times 10 = 1320$.

Method 2:
We use the combination method. We select 3 students from 12 students and we order them: $\binom{12}{3} \times 3! = 1320$.

67. Solution: 450.
$\dfrac{270}{18} = \dfrac{x}{30} \implies x = 450$.

68. Solution: 24.

15

$$\frac{160}{220} = \frac{x}{3300} \quad \Rightarrow \quad x = 2400 \text{ cm} = 24 \text{ m}.$$

69. Solution: 72.
$5x + 7x + 72 = 180 \quad \Rightarrow \quad 12x = 108 \quad \Rightarrow \quad x = 9.$
The two angles are $5 \times 9 = 45$ and $7 \times 9 = 63$.
The measure in degrees of the largest angle in the triangle is 72.

70. Solution: 3,600.

5% of the 250 million is 12.5 million.
$45 billion is 45,000 million.
45,000/12.5 = 3600.

71. Solution: $\frac{3}{8}$.

We have $\frac{4!}{2! \times 2!} = 6$ ways to order HHTT.

The probability is $P = \frac{1}{2} \times \frac{1}{2} \times \frac{1}{2} \times \frac{1}{2} \times 6 = \frac{3}{8}$.

72. Solution: 5/18.
We get 10 pairs: (1, 2), (2, 1), (2, 3), (3, 2), (3, 4) (4, 3), (4, 5), (5, 4), (5, 6), (6, 5).
The probability is 10/36 = 5/18.

73. Solution: 8.
An octagonal prism has $8 + 8 + 8 = 24$ sides. An octagonal pyramid has $8 + 8 = 16$ sides
The difference is $24 - 16 = 8$.

74. Solution: 549.
The first term is 102 and the last term is 996. The number of terms is n.

The sum of these numbers is $S = \frac{(a_1 + a_n)n}{2}$.

The arithmetic mean is $\frac{S}{n} = \frac{(a_1 + a_n)}{2} \quad \Rightarrow \quad \frac{S}{n} = \frac{(102 + 996)}{2} = 549$.

75. Solution: 1/3.

The volume of the cone is $V_1 = \frac{1}{3}\pi r^2 h$.

The volume of the cylinder is $V_2 = \pi r^2 h$.
The ratio is 1/3.

76. Solution: $12\sqrt{3}$.
The 12 equilateral triangles are congruent.
The total area is
$12 \times \frac{\sqrt{3}}{4} a^2 = 12 \times \frac{\sqrt{3}}{4} \times 2^2 = 12\sqrt{3}$.

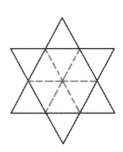

77. Solution: 80%.
$x = \frac{60}{100} \times y$ \hfill (1)

$\frac{m}{100} \times 3y = 4x$ \hfill (2)

(1) × (2): $\frac{m}{100} \times 3y \times x = 4x \times \frac{60}{100} \times y$ $\Rightarrow$ $\frac{m}{100} \times 3 = 4 \times \frac{60}{100}$ $\Rightarrow$
$m = 80$.

78. Solution: 3.
Method 1: Number of students who cannot swim: 52 – 30 = 22.
Number of students who cannot ride bicycle: 52 – 35 = 17.
Number of students who cannot play tennis: 52 – 42 = 10.
At most 22 + 17 + 10 = 49 students cannot play at least one of the three activities.
At least 52 – 49 = 3 students can do all three sports.

Method 2: **The tickets method**
Step 1: Give each student a ticket for each activity he or she likes. 30 + 35 + 42 = 107 tickets are given out.

Step 2: Take away the tickets from them. Students who have 2 or more tickets will give back 2 tickets. Students who have less than 2 tickets will give back all the tickets.

Step 3: Calculate the number of tickets taken back: at most 2 × 52 = 104 tickets were taken back.

Step 4: Calculate the number of tickets that are still in the students hands.
$107 - 104 = 3$.
At this moment, any student who has the ticket will have only one ticket. These students are the ones who like 3 activities. The answer is 3.

79. Solution: 2.

Let x be the number of additional units that are needed. Then $\dfrac{20}{3 \times 10} = \dfrac{50}{(3+x) \cdot 15}$.

Thus, $x = 2$.

80. Solution: 4 pairs.

$$\dfrac{\dfrac{1}{x} + \dfrac{1}{y}}{1 - \dfrac{1}{xy}} = \dfrac{1}{10} \quad \Rightarrow \quad (x-10)(y-10) = 101.$$

The following four ordered pairs of integer numbers are solutions of this equation: (11, 111), (111, 11), (9, −91), (−91, 9).

MATHCOUNTS

■ **Speed and Accuracy Practice Test 2**■

Name
_____

Date
_____

DO NOT BEGIN UNTIL YOU ARE INSTRUCTED TO DO SO.
The test consists of two parts, with each part 40 problems. You will have 15 minutes to complete the part 1 and 25 minutes to complete the part 2. You are not allowed to use calculators, books, or any other aids during this round. Calculations may be done on scratch paper. All answers must be complete, legible, and simplified to lowest terms. Record only final answers. Do each problem as quick as you can. If you finish one problem, go to the next. Do not spend any time to check your answers.

	Total Correct	Scorer's Initials
Part I		
Part II		

©www.mymathcounts.com

Mathcounts Speed and Accuracy Practice Test 2

Part I Problems 1–40

Mathcounts Speed and Accuracy Practice Tests Test 2

1. $743 - 265 =$

2. $299 \times 6 =$

3. Express $\frac{1}{5}$ of 12 as a mixed number.

4. Write $\frac{7}{5}$ as a percent.

5. $37 + 73 + 37 + 73 + 37 =$

6. $56168 \div 13 =$

7. Express $2\frac{3}{8} - \frac{3}{4}$ as a decimal to the nearest thousandths.

8. Express $3\frac{3}{7}\%$ as a common fraction in the simplest form.

9. What is the *GCF* of 18 and 80?

10. $64 \times 215 =$

11. Which is smaller $\frac{5}{7}$ or $\frac{8}{11}$?

12. $113 \times 103 =$

13. $0.48 \times 0.75 =$

14. $74 \times 76 =$

15. $45{,}792 \div 216 =$

16. The complement of a 49° angle is ___°.

17. 5 quarts = ___ pints

18. 18% of 50 =

19. $\frac{17}{40} =$

20. $\sqrt{648 \div 4.5} \times 9 =$

21. If $a = 23$ and $b = -89$, find $a - b$.

22. Express 3.14×10^{-3} as a decimal.

23. 5ft × 18ft × 9ft = ___ yd^3

24. $96 \times 94 =$

25. $\sqrt{15129} =$

26. 4.3 hours = —— minutes

27. Find the number of subsets of $\{\alpha, \beta, \theta, \pi\}$.

28. If $f(x) = 6x - 2$, then $f(-13) =$

29. $19^2 - 17^2 =$

30. $0.25 \times 7384 =$

31. $13 \times 4\frac{9}{13} =$

32. Write 0.777 . . . as a fraction.

33. $7 \div 0.875 =$

34. Find the sum of the roots of $x^2 - 4x - 12 = 0$.

35. Express 0.0625 as a fraction in the simplest form.

36. $90° =$ —— radians

37. Express $33\frac{3}{9}\%$ as a fraction in the simplest form.

38. Expand $(3x - 1)(4x + 3)$

39. Calculate: $(-3a^2b^3)(-5a^3b)$

40. $15^4 =$

Mathcounts Speed and Accuracy Practice Test 2

Part II Problems 41–80

Mathcounts Speed and Accuracy Practice Tests   **Test 2**

41. What is the maximum number of non-overlapping interior regions that can be created by five chords of a circle?

42. Everyone at the party shook hands with everyone else exactly once. If there were a total of 28 handshakes, how many people were at the party?

43. What is the sum of the two products 2014 × 7 and 2014 × 3?

44. If $3^{2x} = 729$, then what is the value of x? Express your answer as a common fraction.

45. What is the largest product of two primes that have a sum of 24?

46. The average of eleven consecutive even integers is 22. What is the sum of the least and greatest of these integers?

47. How many positive integer divisors does 36 have?

48. The area of square $ABCD$ is 8 square units. What is the area, in square units, of circle O, which is circumscribed about the square? Express your answer in terms of π.

49. Find the maximum number of triangles formed by connecting 6 points in the plane.

50. The measure of an exterior angle of a regular polygon is 60 degrees. How many sides does the polygon have?

51. A jackpot for a contest starts at $10,000 and increases 50% after each round. How many dollars is the jackpot worth after four rounds?

Mathcounts Speed and Accuracy Practice Tests Test 2

52. What is the sum of the cubes of the first four odd positive integers?

53. What is the area, in square units, of a square whose sides are the same length as the radius of a circle with a circumference of 10π units?

54. What is the area, in square units, of the triangle bounded by $y = 0$, $y = x$ and $x + y = 1$?

55. What is the last digit of 2014^{2014}?

56. If x and y are positive integers such that $4x + 2y = 36$ and $3y - 2x = 14$, what is the value of $4y$?

57. How many integers are in the solution of the inequality $|x + 4| < 7$?

58. How many positive integers less than 247 are divisible by 13?

59. Using 4 digits 1, 2, 3, and 4 to form two 2-digit numbers. What is the greatest possible product of these two 2-digit numbers?

60. What is the value of the expression $10^2 - 9^2 + 8^2 - 7^2 + 6^2 - 5^2 + 4^2 - 3^2 + 2^2 - 1^2$?

61. Jack takes twice as long to dig a hole as Ken. The two working together can dig a hole in twenty minutes. How many minutes does it take Ken to dig a hole by himself?

62. Point $P(-5, -12)$ is graphed in a coordinate plane. What is the number of units in the distance from point P to the origin?

63. A region consists of an equilateral triangle divided into smaller congruent equilateral triangles. What percent of the region is not shaded?

64. What is the measure, in units, of the hypotenuse of a right triangle with leg lengths of 16 and 30 units?

65. Cathy will randomly choose an integer from the integers 1 to 100, inclusive. If Cathy chooses a multiple of 9, what is the probability she will choose a perfect square? Express your answer as a common fraction.

66. What is the value of x if $7^x + 7^x + 7^x + 7^x + 7^x + 7^x + 7^x = 7^7$?

67. Find the average speed for the round trip if a car travels from town A to town B at 50 miles per hour but returns the same distance at 70 miles per hour. Express your answer as a common fraction.

68. The probability that Chris will win the first set of a tennis match is $\frac{2}{3}$ and that he will win the second is $\frac{1}{2}$. Assuming independence of the two sets, what is the probability that he wins both sets?

69. Two successive discounts of 30% are equivalent to a single discount of what percent?

70. Find $\angle D$ if $\angle A = 24°$, $\angle B = 74°$, and $\angle C = = 22°$.

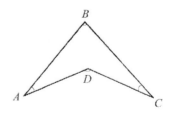

Mathcounts Speed and Accuracy Practice Tests   Test 2

71. The sum of five consecutive integers is 625. What is the third number?

72. A regular octagon is graphed in the coordinate plane. Two adjacent vertices are graphed at (5, 3) and (–1, –5). What is the perimeter of this octagon, in units?

73. What is the remainder when 9^{2015} is divided by 8?

74. Four fair dice are to be rolled. What is the probability that the sum of the four numbers facing up will be 23? Express your answer as a common fraction.

75. In a class of 50 students, 28 take science, 21 take French, and 5 students take both classes. How many students take neither class?

76. What is the smallest number of people you would need to have in a room if you wanted to be certain that at least 11 of them have the same birth month?

77. *ABCD* is a trapezoid. Two diagonals *AC* and *BD* intersect at *E*. Find the area of triangle *ADE* if the area of triangle *BEC* is 4 square units and the area of triangle *ABE* is 9 square units.

78. What is the integer value of $78^2 - 78 \times 106 + 53^2$?

79. If 2 cats can catch 3 mice in 5 days, how many mice can 20 cats catch in 10 days?

80. What is the product of the roots of $x^2 - 40x + 391 = 0$?

Mathcounts Speed and Accuracy Practice Tests — Test 2

Answer Keys

PART I:

1. 478
2. 1794
3. $2\frac{2}{5}$.
4. 140%.
5. 257
6. 432
7. 1.625
8. $\frac{6}{175}$
9. 2
10. 13,760
11. $\frac{5}{7}$
12. 11,639
13. 0.36
14. 5624
15. 212
16. 41°.
17. 10
18. 9
19. 0.425
20. 108
21. 112
22. 0.00314
23. 30
24. 9,024
25. 123
26. 258
27. 16 (subsets)
28. −80
29. 72
30. 1,846
31. 61
32. $\frac{7}{9}$
33. 8.
34. 4.
35. $\frac{1}{16}$
36. $\frac{1}{2}\pi$
37. $\frac{1}{3}$.
38. $12x^2 + 5x - 3$
39. $15a^5b^4$
40. 50625.

Mathcounts Speed and Accuracy Practice Tests   **Test 2**

PART II:

41. 16 (regions)
42. 8 (people)
43. 20140.
44. 3
45. 143
46. 44
47. 9 (divisors)
48. 4π (sq units)
49. 20 (triangles)
50. 6 (sides)
51. 50,625 (dollars)
52. 496.
53. 25 (sq units)
54. 1/4 (sq units)
55. 6
56. 32
57. 13 (integers)
58. 18.
59. 1312.
60. 55.
61. 30 (minutes)

62. 13 (units)
63. 25 (percent)
64. 34 (units)
65. 3/11.
66. 6.
67. $\frac{175}{3}$.
68. $\frac{1}{3}$.
69. 51 (percent)
70. 120°.
71. 125.
72. 80 (units)
73. 1.
74. 1/324.
75. 6 (students).
76. 121 (people)
77. 4 (square units)
78. 625
79. 60
80. 391.

Solutions to Part II:

41. Solution: 16.

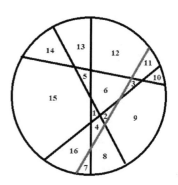

42. Solution: 8.
Since there are two people involved with each handshake, the total number of handshakes the n people will make is $\binom{n}{2} = \frac{n(n-1)}{2}$.

Then we have $\frac{n(n-1)}{2} = 28 \Rightarrow (n-1)n = 2 \times 28 = 7 \times 8$.

So $n = 8$.

43. Solution: 20140.
$2014 \times 7 + 2014 \times 3 = 2014 (7 + 3) = 20140$.

44. Solution: 3.
$3^{2x} = 729 = 3^6 \quad \Rightarrow \quad 2x = 6 \quad \Rightarrow \quad x = 3$.

45. Solution: 143.
$24 = 19 + 5 = 17 + 7 = 13 + 11$.
The largest product is $13 \times 11 = 143$.

46. Solution: 44.
Let a_1 and a_{11} be the first term and the last term.

The sum of these of eleven consecutive even integers $S = \frac{(a_1 + a_{11}) \times 11}{2}$.

The average is $\frac{S}{11} = \frac{a_1 + a_{11}}{2} = 22$. Thus $a_1 + a_{11} = 44$.

47. Solution: 9.
$36 = 6^2 = 2^2 \times 3^2$.

The number of divisors is (2 + 1) (2 + 1) = 9.

48. Solution: 4π.

The side length of the square is $2\sqrt{2}$.

The diagonal of the square is $\sqrt{2} \times 2\sqrt{2} = 4$, which is the diameter of the circle.

The area of the circle is $\frac{1}{4}\pi d^2 = \frac{1}{4}\pi(4)^2 = 4\pi$.

49. Solution: 20.
$\binom{6}{3} = \frac{6 \times 5 \times 4}{3 \times 2 \times 1} = 20$

50. Solution: 6.
The measure of an interior angle of this regular polygon is 180 − 60 = 120 degrees.
$120 = \frac{(n-2) \times 180}{n}$ $\Rightarrow$ $2n = (n-2) \times 3$ $\Rightarrow$ $n = 6$.

51. Solution: $50625.
$10,000 × 1.5^4 = $10,000 × 5.0625 = $50625.

52. Solution: 496.
$1^3 + 3^3 + 5^3 + 7^3 = 1 + 27 + 125 + 343 = 496$.

53. Solution: 25.
The radius of a circle with a circumference of 10π units is r and $2\pi r = 10\pi$. So $r = 5$.
The area of the square is $5^2 = 25$.

54. Solution: $\frac{1}{4}$.

The shaded area is $\dfrac{\frac{1}{2} \times 1 \times 1}{2} = \frac{1}{4}$

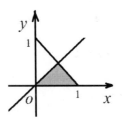

55. Solution: 6.
The last digit of 2014^{2014} is the same as the last digit of 4^{2014}. The last digit of 4^{2014} is the same as the last digit of 4^4, which is 6.

Mathcounts Speed and Accuracy Practice Tests Test 2

56. Solution: 32.
$4x + 2y = 36$ \hfill (1)
$3y - 2x = 14$ \hfill (2)
$(2) \times 2 + (1): 8y = 64 \Rightarrow 4y = 32$.

57. Solution: 13.
$x + 4 < 7 \Rightarrow x < 3$. x can be 2, 1, and 0.
$x + 4 > -7 \Rightarrow x > -11$. x can be $-10, -9, \ldots, -1$.
There are $3 + 10 = 13$ integers.

58. Solution: 18.
$247 = 13 \times 19$.
All the positive integers from 13×1 to 13×18 are divisible by 13. There are 18 of them.

59. Solution: 1312.
The greatest possible product is $41 \times 32 = 1312$.
Note: $42 \times 31 = 1302$.

60. Solution: 55.
$(10^2 - 9^2) + (8^2 - 7^2) + (6^2 - 5^2) + (4^2 - 3^2) + (2^2 - 1^2) = 19 + 15 + 11 + 7 + 3 = 55$.

61. Solution: 30 minutes.
Let K be the time needed for Ken to dig a hole himself, and J be the time needed for Jack to dig a hole along. $J = 2K$.

$(\frac{1}{J} + \frac{1}{K}) \times 20 = 1 \Rightarrow (\frac{1}{2K} + \frac{1}{K}) \times 20 = 1 \Rightarrow \frac{3}{2K} \times 20 = 1 \Rightarrow K = 30$ minutes.

62. Solution: 13.
$d = \sqrt{(-5)^2 + (-12)^2} = 13$.

63. Solution: 25%.
The four equilateral triangles are congruent. The percent of the region not shaded is 1/4 or 25%.

64. Solution: 34.

$\sqrt{16^2+30^2}=34$.

65. Solution: 3/11.

There are $\left\lfloor\dfrac{100}{9}\right\rfloor=11$ numbers that is a multiple of 9. Among them, three are perfect squares (9, 36, and 81). The probability is 3/11.

66. Solution: 6.
$7^x+7^x+7^x+7^x+7^x+7^x+7^x=7\times 7^x=7^{x+1}$.
So $x+1=7 \Rightarrow x=6$.

67. Solution: $\dfrac{175}{3}$.

Let v be the average speed for the entire round trip.
$v=\dfrac{2\times d}{\dfrac{d}{50}+\dfrac{d}{70}}=\dfrac{175}{3}$.

68. Solution: $\dfrac{1}{3}$.

$P=\dfrac{2}{3}\times\dfrac{1}{2}=\dfrac{1}{3}$.

69. Solution: 51%.
Let x be the original price.
After the discounts, the sale price is $(1-0.3)(1-0.3)\times x=0.7\times 0.7x=0.49x$.
The discount is $(1-0.49)=0.51=51\%$.

70. Solution: 120°.
$\angle D=\angle A+\angle B+\angle C=24°+74°+22°=120°$.

71. Solution: 125.
The third number is the average of five consecutive integers. 625/5 = 125.

72. Solution: 80.
The length of one side is $d=\sqrt{(-1-5)^2+(-5-3)^2}=10$.

The perimeter of this octagon is 10 × 8 = 80.

73. Solution: 1.
The remainder when 9^{2015} is divided by 8 is the same as the remainder when 1^{2015} is divided by 8. So the answer is 1.

74. Solution: 1/324.
The number of ways to roll a sum of 23 is the same as the number of arrangements of 6, 6, 6, 5, which is $\frac{4!}{3!} = 4$. The probability is $\frac{4}{6^4} = \frac{1}{324}$.

75. Solution: 6.
Let x be the number of students taking neither class.
$50 - x = 28 + 21 - 5 \implies x = 6$

76. Solution: 121.
There are 12 months (12 holes) in a year. If 10 people (pigeons) were born in the same month, we need to have 120 students for 12 months. Now if we have one more person, no matter what month he/she was born, there are always 10 students born the same month with him/her.
So the smallest number is 120 + 1 = 121.

77. Solution: 4.
Since $AB//DC$, the area of triangle ADE is the same as the area of triangle BEC, which is 4.

78. Solution: 625.
$78^2 - 78 \times 106 + 53^2 = 78^2 - 2 \times 78 \times 53 + 53^2 = (78 - 53)^2 = (25)^2 = 625$.

79. Solution: 60.
Let x be the number of mice 20 cats catch in 10 days. By the proportion: $\frac{3}{2 \times 5} = \frac{x}{20 \times 10}$.
$x = 60$.

80. Solution: 391.
By the Vieta's Theorem, the product of the roots is $\frac{391}{1} = 391$.

MATHCOUNTS

■ **Speed and Accuracy Practice Test 3** ■

Name

Date

DO NOT BEGIN UNTIL YOU ARE INSTRUCTED TO DO SO.
The test consists of two parts, with each part 40 problems. You will have 15 minutes to complete the part 1 and 25 minutes to complete the part 2. You are not allowed to use calculators, books, or any other aids during this round. Calculations may be done on scratch paper. All answers must be complete, legible, and simplified to lowest terms. Record only final answers. Do each problem as quick as you can. If you finish one problem, go to the next. Do not spend any time to check your answers.

	Total Correct	Scorer's Initials
Part I		
Part II		

©www.mymathcounts.com

Mathcounts Speed and Accuracy Practice Test 3

Part I Problems 1–40

Mathcounts Speed and Accuracy Practice Tests   **Test 3**

PART I

1. 95% = ——— fraction

2. $127 \times 25 =$

3. $6\frac{1}{2}\% =$ ——— decimal

4. $\frac{1}{3} + \frac{2}{5} =$ ———

5. $1{,}234{,}567 + 7{,}654{,}321 =$

6. $46 \times 11 =$

7. $32 \div 4 - 4 \times 2 =$

8. $65^2 =$

9. The LCM of 12 and 34 is ———

10. $3{,}249 \div 57 =$

11. $11\frac{5}{7} \times 7 =$

12. $81 \times 101 =$

13. $\frac{5}{6} \times \frac{3}{8} \times \frac{2}{15} =$

14. $24 \times 84 =$

15. $3.8 \times 6.3 + 12.6 \times 3.1 =$

16. $1 + 2 + 3 + \ldots + 99 + 100 =$ ———

17. 2 square feet = ——— square inches.

18. If $7x + 7 = 5x + 9$, then $x =$

19. $103 \times 107 =$

20. $20 \times 22 \times 25 =$

21. $17 \times 8 + 17 \times 42 =$

22. 16 is what % of 40?

23. $276 + 199 =$

24. Express 54_8 as a base ten numeral.

25. $7^6 =$

26. $49 \times 61 =$

Mathcounts Speed and Accuracy Practice Tests — Test 3

27. How many proper fractions are there in lowest terms with denominator 12?

28. What is the geometric mean of 3 and 12?

29. Write $9\frac{5}{7} \times 9\frac{2}{7}$ as a mixed number.

30. $\sqrt{12321} =$

31. Write the repeating decimal $0.\overline{142857}$ as a simplest fraction.

32. Express 74_{10} as a base six numeral.

33. The simple interest on $4800 for 6 months at 8% is $

34. $100 - 81 + 64 - 49 + 36 - 25 + 16 - 9 + 4 - 1 =$

35. $37 + 38 + 39 + 40 + 41 + 42 + 43 =$

36. $2015! \div 2014! =$

37. $9^2 + 27^2 =$

38. $(-5a^2b^3c)(-3abc^3) \div (a^2c^4) =$

39. $(6n + 7)(6n - 7) =$

40. $501 \times 326 =$

Mathcounts Speed and Accuracy Practice Test 3

Part II Problems 41–80

Mathcounts Speed and Accuracy Practice Tests — Test 3

41. If the sum of $0.\overline{5} + 0.0.\overline{5} + 0.00\overline{5}$ is written as a fraction with a denominator of 300, what is the numerator?

42. If $\dfrac{11}{6}(r + s + t) = 187$, what is the average of r, s and t?

43. The measure of the supplement of angle A is three times the measure of the complement of angle A. What is the measure, in degrees, of angle A?

44. In a survey of 100 students who watch television, 24 watch American Idol, 42 watch Lost, and seven watch both. How many of the students surveyed watch neither show?

45. The area of an equilateral triangle is numerically equal to its perimeter. What is the the length of one of its sides, in units? Express your answer in simplest radical form.

46. When the sum of the reciprocals of two distinct positive integers is divided by the sum of the two integers, the result is 1/49. What is the sum of the two integers?

47. If x varies inversely with y and y varies directly with the square of z, then by what positive factor is z multiplied when x is multiplied by one-ninth?

48. How many liters of a 20% alcohol solution must be added to 90 liters of a 50% alcohol solution to form a 45% solution?

49. The side length of square A is 91 cm. The side length of square B is 247 cm. What is the ratio of the area of square A to the area of square B? Express your answer as a common fraction.

50. If n is the smallest integer greater than the reciprocal of $0.\overline{12}$, what is n?

Mathcounts Speed and Accuracy Practice Tests   Test 3

51. The real numbers x, y and z satisfy the equations $x + 2y + 3z = 950$ and $3x + 2y + z = 1450$. What is the sum of x, y and z?

52. How many integers between 100 and 1000 are multiples of 7?

53. If two numbers will be randomly chosen without replacement from {3, 4, 5, 6}, what is the probability that their sum will be 9? Express your answer as a common fraction.

54. I have a pet cat Tiger who climbs stairs either one or three steps at a time. Our staircase has 11 steps. How many different ways can Tiger climb the stairs?

55. How many diagonals does a convex polygon with 21 sides have?

56. Mr. Wang has 35% more students this year than he had last year. He has 54 students this year. How many students did he have last year?

57. Tim and Sally are playing a game in which players are awarded either 7 points or 11 points for a correct answer. What is the greatest score that cannot be attained?

58. How many triangles are there in the figure?

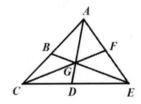

59. ABC is a triangle with side lengths of 7, 24, and 25 centimeters. What is the area of triangle ABC, in square centimeters?

60. If n is a positive integer, what is the smallest value of n for which $\sqrt{\dfrac{27n}{7}}$ is an integer?

Mathcounts Speed and Accuracy Practice Tests Test 3

61. Mr. Lee wishes to donate a sum of money to each of his three favorite charities. His total donation is to be divided among the charities in a ratio of 7:5:3. If his total gift is $15,000, what is the difference, in dollars, between the largest donation and the smallest donation?

62. Three friends have a total of 10 identical pencils, and each one has at least two pencils. In how many ways can this happen?

63. What is the product of all integer values of x for which the value of $|(x-4)(x+2)|$ is a prime number?

64. If the radius of a circle is increased by 10%, by what percent is the area increased?

65. A grocer sells sugar in 4-kg and 7-kg bags. Yesterday he sold 330 kg of sugar using the same number of 4-kg bags as 7-kg bags. What is the total number of bags of sugar that were sold by the grocer yesterday?

66. If five times k is added to 12, the result is 87. What is the value of k^2?

67. When Cathy starts running towards David, David is 90 meters from Cathy. As Cathy runs, David moves directly away from Cathy at one-fourth of Cathy's speed. How far has Cathy run when she first catches up to David?

68. If $1024^4 = 256^x$, what is the value of 2^{-x}? Express your answer as a common fraction.

69. 25% of what number is 30?

70. How many ordered pairs (x, y) satisfy $xy - x + y - 26 = 0$? Both x and y are positive integers.

Mathcounts Speed and Accuracy Practice Tests   Test 3

71. What is the positive cubic root of the product $10 \times 25 \times 32$?

72. Rusty can cut a log into 3 pieces in 20 minutes. At that rate, how long will it take him to cut another such log into 6 pieces?

73. A certain circle's area is x square units, and its circumference is y units. The value of $x + y$ is 120π. What is the radius of the circle, in units?

74. The point (a, b) lies on the line with the equation $3x + 2y = 15$. When $a = 5$, what is the value of b?

75. If 200% of x is equal to 50% of y and $y = 16$, what is the value of x?

76. These figures represent the first four pentagonal numbers. What is the value of the sixth pentagonal number?

                  1 5 12   22

77. What is the sum of the all terms in the arithmetic sequence $-2, -1, 0, 1, 2, 3, ..., 33$?

78. What is the value of $(10! \cdot 5! \cdot 2!) \div (8! \cdot 6!)$?

79. How many ways from A to B with the shortest distance walked if you can walk one step or two steps at a time. Figure shows that there are total 5 steps from A to B.

80. A right circular cone has a volume of 48π cubic centimeters. The height of the cone is 4 cm. How many centimeters is the circumference of the base of the cone, in terms of π?

Mathcounts Speed and Accuracy Practice Tests   **Test 3**

Answer Keys:

PART I

1. $\dfrac{19}{20}$

2. 3175

3. 0.065

4. $\dfrac{11}{15}$

5. 8,888,888

6. 506

7. 0

8. 4225

9. 204

10. 57

11. 82

12. 8181

13. $\dfrac{1}{24}$

14. 2016

15. 63

16. 5050

17. 288

18. 1.

19. 11,021

20. 11,000

21. 850

22. 40

23. 475

24. 44.

25. 117,649

26. 2989

27. 4

28. 6

29. $90\dfrac{10}{49}$

30. 111

31. $\dfrac{1}{7}$.

32. 202_6.

33. $192.

34. 55

35. 280.

36. 2015.

37. 810

38. $15\,ab^4$

39. $36n^2 - 49$

40. 163, 326.

Mathcounts Speed and Accuracy Practice Tests — Test 3

PART II

41. 185.

42. 34.

43. 45 (degrees)

44. 41 (students)

45. 4sqrt 3.

46. 50.

47. 3.

48. 18 liters.

49. 49/361.

50. 9.

51. 600.

52. 128 (integers)

53. 1/3.

54. 41.

55. 189 (diagonals)

56. 40 (students)

57. 59.

58. 16.

59. 84 (sq cm)

60. 21.

61. 4,000 (dollars)

62. 15 ways.

63. 45.

64. 21 (percent).

65. 60 (bags).

66. 225.

67. 120 meters.

68. 1/32.

69. 120.

70. 2.

71. 20.

72. 50 minutes.

73. 10 (units)

74. 0.

75. 4.

76. 51.

77. 558.

78. 30.

79. 35.

80. 12π (centimeters).

Mathcounts Speed and Accuracy Practice Tests — Test 3

Solutions to Part II:

41. Solution: 185.

$$0.\overline{5} + 0.0\overline{5} + 0.00\overline{5} = \frac{5}{9} + \frac{5}{90} + \frac{5}{900} = \frac{500 + 50 + 5}{900} = \frac{555}{900} = \frac{185}{300}$$

42. Solution: 34.

$$\frac{11}{6}(r+s+t) = 187 \implies \frac{1}{6}(r+s+t) = 17 \implies \frac{1}{3}(r+s+t) = 17 \times 2 = 34.$$

43. Solution: 45 (degrees)

$(180° - A) = 3(90° - A) \implies 180° - A = 270° - 3A \implies 3A - A = 270° - 180° \implies 2A = 90° \implies A = 45°.$

44. Solution: 41 (students)

$100 - (24 + 42 - 7) = 41.$

45. Solution: $4\sqrt{3}$.

$$\frac{1}{4}a^2\sqrt{3} = 3a \implies \frac{1}{4}a = \sqrt{3} \implies a = 4\sqrt{3}.$$

46. Solution: 50.

Let two integers be x and y.

$$\frac{\frac{1}{x} + \frac{1}{y}}{x+y} = \frac{1}{49} \implies \frac{\frac{x+y}{xy}}{x+y} = \frac{1}{49} \implies xy = 49.$$

Since two positive integers are distinct, one is 1 and one is 49. So the sum is $1 + 49 = 50$.

47. Solution: 3.

$x = \dfrac{k}{y}$ \hfill (1)

$y = mz^2$ \hfill (2)

46

Substituting (2) into (1): $x = \dfrac{k}{mz^2}$ (3)

Multiplying both sides of (3) by 1/9:

$\dfrac{1}{9}x = \dfrac{k}{mz^2} \times \dfrac{1}{9}$ $\Rightarrow$ $X = \dfrac{k}{m(Z)^2}$, where $Z = 3z$.

48. Solution: 18 liters.

Name	C	V	S
A	0.2	x	0.2 × x
B	0.5	90	45
Mixture	0.45	90 + x	0.45(90 + x)

$0.45(90 + x) = 0.2x + 45$ $\Rightarrow$ $x = 18$ liters.

49. Solution: 49/361.

$\dfrac{S_A}{S_B} = \left(\dfrac{91}{247}\right)^2 = \left(\dfrac{7}{19}\right)^2 = \dfrac{49}{361}$

50. Solution: 9.

$0.\overline{12} = \dfrac{12}{99} = \dfrac{4}{33}$.

The reciprocal is $\dfrac{33}{4} = 8.25$. So n is 9.

51. Solution: 600.
$x + 2y + 3z = 950$ (1)
$3x + 2y + z = 1450$ (2)

(1) + (2): $4x + 4y + 4z = 1450 + 950 = 2400$ $\Rightarrow$ $x + y + z = 600$.

52. Solution: 128 (integers)

$\left\lfloor \dfrac{1000}{7} \right\rfloor - \left\lfloor \dfrac{100}{7} \right\rfloor = 142 - 14 = 128$.

53. Solution: 1/3.

We have $\binom{4}{2} = 6$ ways to select two numbers.

We have two ways to get a sum of 9 by picking up two numbers: (3, 6) and (4, 5). The probability is 2/6 = 1/3.

Method 2:
We can pick up any one number of (3, 4, 5, 6). After we pick up the number, we have 1/3 of chance to match it. So the probability is 1/3.

54. Solution: 41.
Tiger has one way to climb stair 1, 1 way to climb stair 2, and 2 ways to climb stair 3 (1 + 1 + 1, and 3).
With the formula $N_4 = N_3 + N_1$, the sequence is as follows: 1, 1, 2, 3, 4, 6, 9, 13, 19, 28, **41.**
N_1 means that the number of ways the frog can hop up to the stair 1.
N_3 means that the number of ways the frog can hop up to the stair 3.
N_4 means that the number of ways the frog can hop up to the stair 4.

55. Solution: 189 (diagonals)
$$\binom{n}{2} - n = \binom{21}{2} - 21 = \frac{21 \times 20}{2} - 21 = 21(10 - 1) = 21 \times 9 = 189.$$

56. Solution: 40 (students)
$1.35x = 54 \quad \Rightarrow \quad x = 40$.

57. Solution: 59.
$7 \times 11 - (7 + 11) = 59$.

58. Solution: 16.
Solution:

The total number of triangles possibly formed is $\binom{6}{3} = 20$, where 6 represents the total number of lines and we choose any three lines to form a triangle.

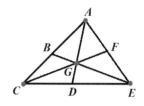

However, choosing three lines meeting at the red dot will form a degenerate triangle, meaning it won't form a triangle. There are $4 \times \binom{3}{3} = 4$ such degenerate triangles.

The desired solution is then $20 - 4 = 16$.

59. Solution: 84 (sq cm).

Note that 7, 24, 25 is a Pythagorean Triple. The area is then $\frac{7 \times 24}{2} = 7 \times 12 = 84$.

60. Solution: 21.

$\sqrt{\frac{27n}{7}} = 3\sqrt{\frac{3n}{7}} = 3\sqrt{\frac{3 \times 3 \times 7}{7}} = 9$. So $n = 3 \times 7 = 21$.

61. Solution: 4,000 (dollars)

$\frac{7}{7+5+3} \times 15000 - \frac{3}{7+5+3} \times 15000 = \frac{4}{15} \times 15000 = 4,000$.

62. Solution: 15 ways.
We distribute 2 balls to each person first to meet the restriction that each person gets two balls.

Now we have 4 balls left. The answer is the number of nonnegative solutions to the following equation: $a + b + c + d = 4$. The answer is $\binom{4+3-1}{3-1} = \binom{6}{2} = 15$

63. Solution: 45.
Let $x - 4 = 1$ $\Rightarrow$ $x = 5$, and $|(x-4)(x+2)| = 7$ (prime number)
Let $x - 4 = -1$ $\Rightarrow$ $x = 3$, and $|(x-4)(x+2)| = 5$ (prime number)
Let $x + 2 = 1$ $\Rightarrow$ $x = -1$, and $|(x-4)(x+2)| = 5$ (prime number)
Let $x + 2 = -1$ $\Rightarrow$ $x = -3$, and $|(x-4)(x+2)| = 7$ (prime number)

So the product is $5 \times 3 \times (-1) \times (-3) = 45$.

64. Solution: 21 (percent).

Mathcounts Speed and Accuracy Practice Tests   Test 3

Solution:
$$\frac{S_1}{S_2} = (\frac{1.1r_1}{r_1})^2 = 1.21.$$
The answer is 21%.

65. Solution: 60 (bags).
$4x + 7y = 330$ ⇒ $11x = 330$ ⇒ $x = 30$ and $y = x = 30$.
So the answer is $30 + 30 = 60$.

66. Solution: 225.
$5k + 12 = 87$ ⇒ $5k = 75$ ⇒ $k = 15$ ⇒ $k^2 = 225$.

67. Solution: 120 meters.
$(V_C - V_D)t = 90$ ⇒ $(V_C - \frac{V_C}{4})t = 90$ ⇒ $\frac{3V_C}{4}t = 90$ ⇒ $V_C \times t = 120$.

68. Solution: 1/32.
$1024^4 = 256^x$ ⇒ $2^{40} = 2^{8x}$ ⇒ $x = 5$ ⇒ $2^{-x} = 2^{-5} = \frac{1}{2^5} = \frac{1}{32}$.

69. Solution: 120.
$\frac{25}{100} \times x = 30$ ⇒ $x = 120$.

70. Solution: 2.
$xy - x + y - 26 = 0$ ⇒ $(x+1)(y-1) = 25$.
If $x+1=1$, $y-1=25$. We get one pair: (0, 26) (ignored since x must be positive integer).
If $x+1=25$, $y-1=1$. We get one pair: (24, 2).
If $x+1=5$, $y-1=5$. We get one pair: (4, 6). The answer is 2.

71. Solution: 20.
$10 \times 25 \times 32 = 2 \times 5 \times 5^2 \times 2^5 = 5^3 \times (2^2)^3 = (5 \times 2^2)^3$.
So the answer is $5 \times 2^2 = 20$.

72. Solution: 50 minutes.
As shown in the figure, only 2 cuts are needed to cut the log into 3 pieces.

Mathcounts Speed and Accuracy Practice Tests   Test 3

   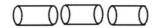

So it takes 10 minutes to saw through the log. To get 6 pieces you will make 5 cuts at 10 minutes each.

73. Solution: 10 (units)
$\pi r^2 = x$
$2\pi r = y$
$\pi r^2 + 2\pi r = x + y = 120\pi \Rightarrow r^2 + 2r = 120 \Rightarrow r^2 + 2r - 120 = 0 \Rightarrow$
$(r-10)(r+12) = 0 \Rightarrow r = 10$.

74. Solution: 0.
$3x + 2y = 15 \Rightarrow 3a + 2b = 15 \Rightarrow 3 \times 5 + 2b = 15 \Rightarrow b = 0$.

75. Solution: 4.
$200\% \times x = 50\% \times y \Rightarrow 4x = y \Rightarrow 4x = 16 \Rightarrow x = 4$.

76. Solution: 51.

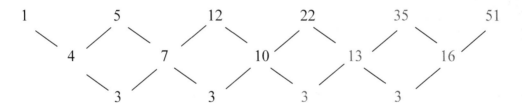

77. Solution: 558.
$a_n = a_1 + (n-1)d \Rightarrow 33 = -2 + (n-1) \times 1 \Rightarrow n = 36$.
$S_n = \dfrac{(a_1 + a_n)n}{2} = \dfrac{(-2+33) \times 36}{2} = 558$

78. Solution: 30.
$\dfrac{10! \cdot 5! \cdot 2!}{8! \cdot 6!} = \dfrac{10 \cdot 9 \cdot 8! \cdot 5! \cdot 2!}{8! \cdot 6!} = \dfrac{10 \cdot 9 \cdot 5! \times 2!}{6!} = \dfrac{10 \cdot 9 \cdot 5! \cdot 2!}{6 \cdot 5!} = \dfrac{10 \cdot 9 \cdot 2}{6} = 30$

79. Solution: 35.
We count the number of rows (3) and the number of columns (4).
So we have $\binom{4+3}{3} = 35$ routes.

80. Solution: 12π (centimeters).
$\dfrac{\pi r^2 h}{3} = 48\pi \quad \Rightarrow \quad \dfrac{r^2 \times 4}{3} = 48 \quad \Rightarrow \quad r = 6$.
The circumference is $2\pi r = 2\pi \times 6 = 12\pi$.

MATHCOUNTS

■ **Speed and Accuracy Practice Test 4**■

Name
_____

Date
_____

DO NOT BEGIN UNTIL YOU ARE INSTRUCTED TO DO SO.
The test consists of two parts, with each part 40 problems. You will have 15 minutes to complete the part 1 and 25 minutes to complete the part 2. You are not allowed to use calculators, books, or any other aids during this round. Calculations may be done on scratch paper. All answers must be complete, legible, and simplified to lowest terms. Record only final answers. Do each problem as quick as you can. If you finish one problem, go to the next. Do not spend any time to check your answers.

	Total Correct	Scorer's Initials
Part I		
Part II		

©www.mymathcounts.com

Mathcounts Speed and Accuracy Practice Test 4

Part I Problems 1–40

Mathcounts Speed and Accuracy Practice Tests   Test 4

1. $38 + 250 + 212 =$

2. Write $152 \div 7$ as a mixed number

3. $23 \times 23 =$

4. $6 \times 998 =$ ——

5. $4 \times 39 =$

6. Write $\dfrac{17}{25}$ as a decimal to the nearest hundredths.

7. $3 \div 0.375 =$

8. Which is larger $\dfrac{7}{12}$ or $\dfrac{5}{8}$?

9. 16 inches = —— feet. Express the answer as a common fraction.

10. 52 quarters minus 4 dimes = $

11. $(24 \times 8) - (12 \times 4) =$

12. $(73 - 37) \div 9$ has a remainder of ——

13. $\sqrt{1369} =$

14. $(-16) + 11 - (-15) =$

15. Write the length of a rectangle with width 4.5 and perimeter 24 as a mixed number.

16. If a quart of milk costs $3.29, then 2 gallons costs $ ——

17. $5\dfrac{1}{3} \times 24 =$

18. $3\dfrac{2}{5} \times 17\dfrac{2}{5} =$ —— mixed number.

19. Write the fraction equivalent to $62\dfrac{1}{2}\%$.

20. If $a = 24$, $b = -4$ and $c = -2$, then $-\dfrac{ac}{b} =$

21. The mode of 13, 3, 13, 33, 32, 12 and 13 is

22. Evaluate $29 \times 31 + 19 \times 21$

23. Find the product of the LCM and the GCF of 15 and 16.

Mathcounts Speed and Accuracy Practice Tests — Test 4

24. What is the area of a square with side $3\sqrt{14}$?

25. $28^2 - 27^2 =$

26. What is the number of proper subsets of $\{\Delta, \pi, \beta, \theta, \omega\}$?

27. Express $\dfrac{18}{15} \times 18$ as a decimal to the nearest tenths.

28. 45% of 9 is 5% of what number?

29. If $f(x) = -4(x-3)^2$, then $f(-5) =$

30. What is the probability of getting ten heads when flipping 10 coins? Express the answer as a common fraction.

31. The slope of the line passing through $(0, -5)$ and $(-5, 10)$ is

32. $73 \times 77 =$

33. The difference between the sum the exterior angle and the sum of interior angles of a right triangle is —°

34. $997 \times 993 =$ —

35. $45 \times 3367 =$

36. The distance between $(4, 6)$ and $(11, 30)$ is ——

37. 50° Fahrenheit = —— °Celsius

38. Find the value of $51^2 - 49^2 + 101^2 - 99^2 = $.

39. The diagonal of a square with side $\sqrt{14}$ is ——

40. $\sqrt{3721} =$

Mathcounts Speed and Accuracy Practice Test 4

Part II Problems 41–80

Mathcounts Speed and Accuracy Practice Tests Test 4

41. If the four points (1, 7), (6, −3), (−1, 11) and (6, y) lie on a line, what is the value of y?

42. If Lily rolls two standard, six-sided dice once, what is the probability that she will roll a sum of 2, 3 or 10? Express your answer as a common fraction.

43. What is the value of $7^2 - 7^3$?

44. If Alex can run at a rate of 704 feet per minute, what is his speed, in miles per hour?

45. What is the mean of {23, 25, 27, 29, 31}?

46. What is the sum of the prime factors of 410?

47. Betsy is nine years older than her sister. In four years, Betsy will be twice as old as her sister will be. In years, how old is Betsy now?

48. A square is surrounded by four equilateral triangles, as shown. Find the total area of the five regions if the side length of the square is 2 cm. Express your answer in simplest radical form.

49. Alex ran 9 kilometers in 30 minutes. What was his average speed, in meters per second? Express your answer as a mixed number.

50. What is the sum of all positive divisors of 4^5?

Mathcounts Speed and Accuracy Practice Tests Test 4

51. A spinner has 15 congruent sections colored either black or red. If the spinner lands on a black section 17 out of 85 spins, what would be the best prediction for the number of sections that are colored red?

52. A botanist found that a certain forest contains only pine, spruce, oak and maple trees. These trees appear in a ratio of 3:5:7:9, respectively. Out of 2,016 trees in this forest, how many would be expected to be oak trees?

53. There are 10 marbles in a bag, some green and the rest red. Whenever three of marbles are removed from the bag, at least one of the marbles is green. How many red marbles are in the bag?

54. What is the smallest positive difference between two integers whose product is 2015?

55. A right triangle has a hypotenuse of length 17 cm and one leg of length 8 cm. The other leg of the triangle is the diameter of a semicircle, as shown. What is the area of the semicircle, in square centimeters? Express your answer in terms of π.

56. What is $2015^2 - 2013^2$?

57. Mary averaged 95 points on her first three tests. If she averages 90 points on her next two tests, what will her average be for all five tests?

58. A rectangle has area 1296 cm², and its length is four times its width. What is the perimeter of the rectangle, in centimeters?

59. The number 585 can be written as the sum of two consecutive integers, 292 and 293. What is the greatest number of consecutive positive integers whose sum is 585?

60. A circle of radius 2 inches has its center at C and is tangent to the sides of a square. Two points A and B are drawn, each on the square midway between a point of tangency of the circle and one vertex of the square. What is the area of triangle ABC, in square inches? Express your answer as a common fraction.

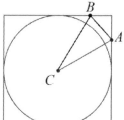

61. The Skate Sports Store offers 4-wheel and 5-wheel inline skates. If there are 84 wheels and 19 different styles of skates in the display, how many of the displayed skates have 5 wheels?

62. What is the greatest possible odd integer less than 2015 that is divisible by both 9 and 11?

63. Find x if $\dfrac{2x-y}{5} = \dfrac{x+y}{10} = \dfrac{3}{5}$.

64. Mr. Paterson rolls two standard, six-sided dice. What is the probability that he gets a square number on one of the dice and an even number on the other? Express your answer as a common fraction.

65. If the length of a rectangle is increased by 30% and its width is decreased by 30%, by what percent is the area decreased?

66. In how many ways can 65¢ be made using any possible combination of quarters, dimes, and nickels? Your combinations need to have at least one coin of each kind.

67. In how many ways can 5 different books be arranged on a shelf if two of the books must remain together, but may be interchanged?

Mathcounts Speed and Accuracy Practice Tests Test 4

68. John has a total of $2.40 in nickels and dimes, with twice as many nickels as there are dimes. How many nickels does John have?

69. In a list of 12 numbers, four of the numbers are increased by 4, and four of the numbers are increased by 5. By how much is the mean increased?

70. What is the largest positive integer that is a factor of every 4-digit odd palindrome?

71. Quadrilateral $ABCD$ is inscribed in a circle, as shown. If $\angle A = 90°$, $CD = 10$ cm and $BD = 26$ cm, what is the area of triangle BCD, in square centimeters?

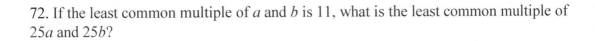

72. If the least common multiple of a and b is 11, what is the least common multiple of $25a$ and $25b$?

73. Suppose 2 sides of a triangle have lengths 19 cm and 31 cm. Find the number of possible integer lengths of the third side.

74. What is the product of 297 and $0.\overline{71}$?

75. Given that $33 \leq n \leq 66$ and $22 \leq d \leq 99$, what is the product of the smallest and largest possible values for the fraction n/d?

Mathcounts Speed and Accuracy Practice Tests   **Test 4**

76. If $5x + 7 = 15 - 2y$, what is the value of $15x + 6y$?

77. How many sides does a polygon have if the sum of the measures of the interior angles is 362160 degrees?

78. What common fraction is equivalent to $0.2\overline{54}$?

79. In the plane figure, only downward motion (movement leaving you relatively lower than where you were) is allowed. Find the total number of paths from A to B.

80. A movie that starts at 7:45 pm is 3 hours, 28 minutes long. What time will the movie end?

Mathcounts Speed and Accuracy Practice Tests Test 4

Answer Keys :

Part I:

1. 500

2. $21\frac{5}{7}$

3. 529

4. 5988

5. 156

6. 0.68.

7. 8

8. $\frac{5}{8}$

9. $\frac{4}{3}$

10. 12.60

11. 144

12. 0

13. 37

14. 10

15. $7\frac{1}{2}$.

16. 26.32

17. 128

18. $59\frac{4}{25}$

19. 5/8.

20. −12.

21. 13

22. 1298

23. 240.

24. 126.

25. 55

26. 31

27. 21.6.

28. 81

29. − 256

30. $\frac{1}{1024}$.

31. − 3.

32. 5621

33. 180°.

34. 990,021

35. 151,515

36. 25

37. 10

38. 600.

39. $2\sqrt{7}$

40. 61

Mathcounts Speed and Accuracy Practice Tests   Test 4

PART II

41. −3.

42. 1/6.

43. − 294

44. 8 (mi/h).

45. 27

46. 48.

47. 14.

48. $4\sqrt{3} + 4$.

49. 5 m/s

50. 2047

51. 12.

52. 588.

53. 2.

54. 34.

55. 8π (cm^2)

56. 8056.

57. 93.

58. 180 cm.

59. 30.

60. 3/2.

61. 8.

62. 1881.

63. 3.

64. 11/36

65. 9%

66. 4.

67. 48.

68. 24.

69. 3.

70. 11.

71. 120 cm^2.

72. 275.

73. 37.

74. 213.

75. 1.

76. 24.

77. 2014.

78. 14/55

79. Solution: 11.

80. 11:13 pm.

Mathcounts Speed and Accuracy Practice Tests Test 4

Solutions to Part II:

41. Solution: −3.
$$\frac{-3-7}{6-1} = \frac{11-(-3)}{1-6} = \frac{y-11}{6-(-1)} = -2 \quad \Rightarrow \quad y = -3.$$

42. Solution: 1/6.
2 = 1 + 1
3 = 1 + 2 = 2 + 1
10 = 6 + 4 = 4 + 6 = 5 + 5.
The probability is $P = \frac{6}{36} = \frac{1}{6}$.

43. Solution: − 294
$7^2 − 7^3 = 7^2 (1 − 7) = 49 \times (−6) = (50 − 1) \times (−6) = − 300 + 6 = − 294$.

44. Solution: 8 (mi/h).
$$\frac{704 \times 60}{5280} = 8.$$

45. Solution: 27
We see that 23, 25, 27, 29, 31 form an arithmetic sequence. The mean is the middle number. So the answer is 27.

46. Solution: 48.
410 = 41 × 2 × 5.
41 + 2 + 5 = 48.

47. Solution: 14.
$B = 9 + S$ (1)
$B + 4 = 2(S + 4)$ (2)

Substituting (1) into (2): $S = 5$.
So $B = 9 + S = 9 + 5 = 14$.

48. Solution: $4\sqrt{3} + 4$.

Mathcounts Speed and Accuracy Practice Tests   Test 4

The area of each triangle is $\frac{1}{4} \times a^2 \times \sqrt{3} = \frac{1}{4} \times 2^2 \times \sqrt{3} = \sqrt{3}$.

So the total area is $4\sqrt{3} + 4$.

49. Solution: 5 m/s

$\frac{9 \times 1000}{30 \times 60} = 5$.

50. Solution: 2047.

$4^5 = 2^{10}$.

The sum of all positive divisors $2^{10} + 2^9 + 2^8 + 2^7 + 2^6 + 2^5 + 2^4 + 2^3 + 2^2 + 2^1 + 2^0 =$
$1024 + 512 + 256 + 128 + 64 + 32 + 16 + 8 + 4 + 2 + 1 = 2047$.

Or by the formula: $S_n = \frac{a_1 - a_n q}{1 - q}$ $\Rightarrow$ $S = \frac{2^{10} - 1 \times \frac{1}{2}}{1 - \frac{1}{2}} = 2047$

51. Solution: 12.

$\frac{85 - 17}{85} \times 15 = 12$.

52. Solution: 588.

$\frac{7}{3 + 5 + 7 + 9} \times 2016 = 588$.

53. Solution: 2.
If we have 3 red marble, we could pick up them so we cannot get a green marble.
So at most we can have two red marbles.

54. Solution: 34.
We write 2015 as the product of two numbers that are as close as possible to get the smallest difference: $2015 = 5 \times 13 \times 31 = 65 \times 31$
$65 - 31 = 34$.

55. Solution: 8π (cm^2)
The triangle is a 8-15-17 right triangle. The radius of the circle is 8/2 = 4. The area of the semicircle, in square centimeters, is 8π.

56. Solution: 8056.
$2015^2 - 2013^2 = (2015 - 2013)(2015 + 2013) = 2 \times 4028 = 8056$.

57. Solution: 93.
$$\frac{95 \times 3 + 90 \times 2}{5} = 93$$

58. Solution: 180 cm.
The width is 18 and the length is 4×18. The perimeter is $18 + 18 + 4 \times 18 + 4 \times 18 = 18 \times 10 = 180$.

59. Solution: 30.

$(2m + k - 1) \times k = 2N$

We need to write $2N$ as the product of two integers that are as close as possible in order to obtain the greatest number with $k < 2m + k - 1$.

$2N = 2 \times 585 = 1170 = 2 \times 3^2 \times 5 \times 13 = 30 \times 39$

Since k is the smaller value of the two factors, $k = 30$.

60. Solution: 3/2.
We label the tangent points as E and F as shown.
The area of triangle ABC = The area of square $ABCD$
− The area of triangle BCE − The area of triangle ACF The area of triangle ABD = $4 - 1 - 1 - 1/2 = 3/2$.

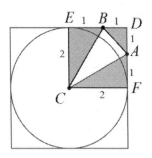

61. Solution: 8.
Let x be the number of 4-wheel inline skates and y be the number of 5-wheel inline skates.
$4x + 5y = 94$ (1)
$x + y = 19$ (2)
$(1) - 4 \times (2)$: $y = 8$.

Mathcounts Speed and Accuracy Practice Tests   Test 4

62. Solution: 1881.
The number is divisible by $9 \times 11 = 99$.
$2015 = 99 \times 20 + 35$.
The greatest number divisible by 99 is $99 \times 20 = 1980$. Since the number must be odd, so it is $1980 - 99 = 1881$.

63. Solution: 3.

$$\frac{2x-y}{5} = \frac{x+y}{10} = \frac{(2x-y)+(x+y)}{15} = \frac{3x}{15} = \frac{3}{5} \quad \Rightarrow \quad x = 3.$$

64. Solution: 11/36

D_2 \ D_1	1	2	3	4	5	6
1	**1,1**	1,2	**1,3**	1,4	**1,5**	1,6
2	2,1	**2,2**	**2,3**	2,4	**2,5**	**2,6**
3	**3,1**	**3,2**	**3,3**	**3,4**	**3,5**	**3,6**
4	4,1	4,2	**4,3**	4,4	**4,5**	4,6
5	**5,1**	**5,2**	**5,3**	**5,4**	**5,5**	**5,6**
6	6,1	**6,2**	**6,3**	6,4	**6,5**	**6,6**

65. Solution: 9%
$1.3 \times 0.7 = 0.91$
Decrease by $1 - 0.91 = 0.09 = 9\%$.

66. Solution: 4.
$25q + 10d + 5n = 65 \quad \Rightarrow \quad 5q + 2d + n = 13.$

q is at most 2. For $q = 2$, $d = 1$ and $n = 1$.

For $q = 1$, $2d + n = 8$. n can be 2, 4, or 6.
So we have total $1 + 3 = 4$ combinations.

67. Solution: 48.
We tie these two books, say book A and book B together, and treat them as one book. Our problem becomes to arrange 4 books on a shelf without restriction:

$$\underline{4} \times \underline{3} \times \underline{2} \times \underline{1} = 4! = 24.$$

Then we un-tie these two books and switch their position (AB $\Rightarrow$ BA), the answer will then be: $2 \times 24 = 48$.

68. Solution: 24.
$10d + 5n = 240$ \hfill (1)
$2d = n$ \hfill (2)
Substituting (2) into (1): $5n + 5n = 240$ $\Rightarrow$ $n = 24$.

69. Solution: 3.
$$\frac{a_1 + a_2 + \cdots a_{12}}{12} = m$$
$$\frac{a_1 + a_2 + \cdots a_{12} + 4 \times 4 + 5 \times 5}{12} = \frac{a_1 + a_2 + \cdots a_{12}}{12} + \frac{36}{12} = m + 3.$$
So the mean increased by 3.

70. Solution: 11.
Let the 4-digit odd palindrome be $\overline{abba}$.
$\overline{abba} = 1000a + 100b + 10b + a = 1001a + 110b = 11(91a + 10b)$.
So every 4-digit odd palindrome is divisible by 11.

71. Solution: 120 cm^2.
Since $\angle A = 90°$, BD is the diameter and $\angle C = 90°$.
Triangle BCD is a 10-24-26 right triangle.
So the area of triangle BCD is:
$24 \times 10/2 = 120$ cm^2.

72. Solution: 275.
$[25a, 25b] = 25[a,b] = 25 \times 11 = 275$.

73. Solution: 37.
Let x be the length of third side.
By the triangle inequality theorem, $31 - 19 < x < 31 + 19$ $\Rightarrow$ $12 < x < 50$.
The possible integer lengths of the third side are ranged from 13 to 49: $49 - 13 + 1 = 37$.

74. Solution: 213.
$297 \times 0.\overline{71} = 297 \times \dfrac{71}{99} = 213$.

75. Solution: 1.
The smallest possible values for the fraction n/d: 33/99.
The largest possible values for the fraction n/d: 66/22.
The product is $\dfrac{33}{99} \times \dfrac{66}{22} = 1$.

76. Solution: 24.
$5x + 7 = 15 - 2y$ $\Rightarrow$ $5x + 2y = 8$ $\Rightarrow$ $3(5x + 2y) = 8 \times 3 = 24$.

77. Solution: 2014.
$(n - 2) \times 180 = 362160$ $\Rightarrow$ $n - 2 = 2012$ $\Rightarrow$ $n = 2014$

78. Solution: 14/55
$0.2\overline{54} = \dfrac{254 - 2}{990} = \dfrac{14}{55}$.

79. Solution: 11.

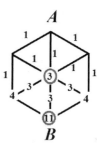

80. Solution: 11:13 pm.
$7 + 3 = 10$.
45 minutes + 28 minutes = 1 hour 13 minutes. So the time will be 11:13 pm.

MATHCOUNTS

■ Speed and Accuracy Practice Test 5■

Name

Date

DO NOT BEGIN UNTIL YOU ARE INSTRUCTED TO DO SO.
The test consists of two parts, with each part 40 problems. You will have 15 minutes to complete the part 1 and 25 minutes to complete the part 2. You are not allowed to use calculators, books, or any other aids during this round. Calculations may be done on scratch paper. All answers must be complete, legible, and simplified to lowest terms. Record only final answers. Do each problem as quick as you can. If you finish one problem, go to the next. Do not spend any time to check your answers.

	Total Correct	Scorer's Initials
Part I		
Part II		

©www.mymathcounts.com

Mathcounts Speed and Accuracy Practice Test 5

Part I Problems 1–40

Mathcounts Speed and Accuracy Practice Tests Test 5

1. 673 − 257 =

2. Write 118 ÷ 9 as a mixed number.

3. 8442 ÷ 4 has remainder of ——

4. 1.25 + 2.2 + 3.75 + 1.8 = ——

5. 3872 + 300 + 1828 =

6. $1.5 \times \frac{4}{3} =$

7. 0.18 km = —— cm

8. The range of 3, 7, 1, 10 and 19 is

9. $7.\overline{6}$ yards = —— feet

10. 367 × 183 =

11. Express 12.5% as a common fraction in simplest form.

12. Calculate 3.5 ÷ 125 to the nearest thousandths.

13. $\frac{4}{14} + \frac{6}{21} + \frac{8}{28} =$ ——

14. (1987 − 1978) ÷ 9 has a remainder of ——

15. 999999 ÷ 7 = ——

16. If $a = -7$, $b = -2$ and $c = -6$, then $-ca \div b =$ ——

17. The supplement of a 73° is —— °

18. The radius of a circle with circumference 22π is ——

19. 112 × 108 = ——

20. 73% of 5700 is

21. The base of a triangle with area 153 and height 9 is ——

22. If $x^3 = -27$, then $x =$

23. 12% of 30 is 3% of ——

24. One mile = —— yards

25. $14 \times 0.\overline{142857} =$

26. 51 × 49 = ——

Mathcounts Speed and Accuracy Practice Tests   **Test 5**

27. The number of permutations of 6 items taken 3 at a time——

28. How many positive, proper fractions are there in lowest terms with denominator 9?

29. The slope of the line $3x + 11y = 25$ is ——

30. $\sqrt{5929}$ = ——

31. Write $\dfrac{27}{40}$ as a decimal to the nearest thousandths.

32. Write 123_5 is base 10.

33. $8^2 + 24^2$ = ——

34. The diagonal of a square with side $\dfrac{\sqrt{2}}{2}$ is ——

35. 22 ft/sec = —— mi/hr

36. $7\dfrac{5}{7} \div 54 \times 133$ =

37. $(8a^4bc^2)(-5a^{-2}bc^{-2})$ =

38. $\sqrt{1024}$ =

39. An icosahedrons has —— faces

40. 5^5 =

Mathcounts Speed and Accuracy Practice Test 5

Part II Problems 41–80

Mathcounts Speed and Accuracy Practice Tests　　　　　　　　　　　　**Test 5**

41. What is the reciprocal of the sum of the reciprocals of 3 and 7? Express your answer as a common fraction.

42. If $\dfrac{a^2}{b} = 1$, then what is the value of $a^2 - b + 1$?

43. If Mary's first three test scores are 92, 89 and 100, what score must she make on the next test to have a test average of 93?

44. Lu began reading a 220-page book at 1:25 pm, and he had read 50 pages by 2:05 pm. If he continues to read at the same rate, how many minutes will it take him to read the remainder of the book?

45. The smallest angle of a triangle measures 30°. What would the degree measure of the smallest angle of the triangle be if the length of each side were tripled?

46. If Lei slices a pie into 25 congruent pieces and then eats 6 pieces, what percent of the pie is left?

47. How many different positive four-digit integers can be formed if the four digits 2, 0, 1, and 4 must be used in each of the integers?

48. What number multiplied by 9 is equal to one more than itself? Express your answer as a common fraction.

49. If $a - x + c = -y + b$ and $x = y - 2c$, what is the value of $a - b$? Express your answer in terms of c.

50. There are 4 red balls, 7 yellow balls, and 8 black balls in a bag. At least how many balls are needed to be taken out randomly in order to guarantee getting 6 balls of the same color?

51. Mary chooses an integer at random from 1 to 100, inclusive. What is the probability that the integer she chooses is a prime number? Express your answer as a common fraction.

52. What is the positive difference between the number of degrees in the smaller angle formed by the hour and minute hands of a clock at 3 p.m. and the smaller angle formed by the hour and minute hands at 6 p.m.?

53. Square $ABCD$ is partitioned into nine congruent squares, with the center square partitioned again into nine congruent squares. What fractional part of square $ABCD$, shown here, is not gray? Express your answer as a common fraction.

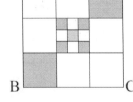

54. Point $(k, -5)$ lies on the line whose equation is $x - 4y = -3$. What is the value of k?

55. What is the slope of the line $3x + 2y = 2$? Express your answer as a common fraction.

56. What is the number of degrees the minute hand of a clock moves between 6:06 p.m. and 6:22 p.m.?

57. What is the remainder when $13^{13} + 5$ is divided by 6?

58. A pencil and seven paper clips weigh the same as three erasers. A pencil weighs the same as 23 paper clips. How many paper clips weigh the same as two erasers?

59. The measure of the area of a trapezoid is numerically equal to eleven times the sum of the lengths of its two bases. What is the height of the trapezoid, in units?

60. If $7a + 11b = 100$, both a and b are positive integers, what is the value of $a + b$?

61. For the first half of a car trip, Alex drove at 60 miles per hour for 2 hours. During the second half of the trip, he drove at half his original speed for twice as long before returning to his starting point. Find Alex's average speed, in miles per hour, for the entire trip.

62. A wire of uniform diameter and composition that weighs 64 lb is cut into two pieces. One piece is 110 yd long and weighs 40 lb. What is the length, in yards, of the original wire?

63. Mr. Raleigh bought a bag of 250 rubber bands for a class project. He has 27 students, and the difference between the numbers of rubber bands any two students received is less than 2. How many students received more rubber bands than others?

64. If one fair coin is tossed five times, what is the probability to get two heads and three tails? Express your answer as a common fraction.

65. Square $ABCD$ is partitioned into four smaller congruent squares, and then portions of those squares are gray, as shown. All segments in the figure marked with double-hash marks are congruent. What fractional part of square $ABCD$ is white? Express your answer as a common fraction.

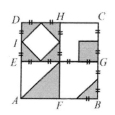

Mathcounts Speed and Accuracy Practice Tests — Test 5

66. Bob makes 3-legged stools and 4-legged chairs, and each requires one seat. One day he used 20 legs. How many chairs did he make?

67. A model of a building is constructed such that the ratio of the dimensions of the model to the dimensions of the building is 1:5. What is the ratio of the volume of the model to the volume of the building? Express your answer as a common fraction.

68. A new rectangle is created by increasing the length and width of the original rectangle by three units each. The numerical value of the area of the new rectangle is equal to m more than the sum of the numerical values of the original rectangle's area and perimeter. What is the value of m if the sum of the length and width of the original rectangle is 2006?

69. When a choir is arranged in rows of five people each, the last row is two persons short. When a choir is arranged in rows of six people each, the last row is still short two persons. What is the least possible number of people in the choir?

70. What is the value of $29 \times 31 + 19 \times 21 + 2$?

71. What is the maximum possible product of two integers whose sum is 62?

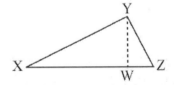

72. In $\triangle XYZ$, $\angle Y = 90°$. $XY = 17$ cm, and $XW = 15$ cm and $YZ = 10$ cm. YW is the altitude from Y to the side XZ. Find $XW \times WZ$.

73. In how many ways can two standard six-sided dice, one red and one white, be rolled to yield a sum that is a multiple of 3?

74. Betty has 39 coins in nickels and quarters. She has nine more quarters than nickels. What is the value of Betty's collection of coins, in dollars? Express your answer as a decimal to the nearest hundredth.

75. A bag contains marbles of four different colors with at least four marbles of each color. Four marbles are randomly selected, without replacement. How many different color combinations are possible? (Note: "red, blue, white, yellow" and "red, blue, yellow, white" are the same combination.)

76. If 65 cards can be copied in 35 minutes, how many hours will it take to copy 780 cards, at the same rate?

77. What is the sum of the number of faces and the number of edges in a regular hexagonal prism?

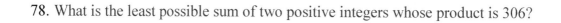

78. What is the least possible sum of two positive integers whose product is 306?

79. Eleven distinct points are drawn on the circumference of a circle. What is the total number of chords that can be drawn connecting any two of these points?

80. Alex has 6 red balls and 4 green balls. How many ways are there such that Alex can arrange them in a row so that no two green balls are next to each other?

Mathcounts Speed and Accuracy Practice Tests   Test 5

Answer Keys :

Part I:

1. 416

2. $13\frac{1}{9}$

3. 2

4. 9

5. 6000

6. 2

7. 18,000

8. 18

9. 23

10. 67,161

11. $\frac{1}{8}$

12. 0.028

13. $\frac{6}{7}$

14. 0

15. 142857

16. 21

17. 107°

18. 11

19. 12,096

20. 4161

21. 34

22. −3.

23. 120

24. 1760

25. 2

26. 2499

27. 20

28. 6

29. $-\frac{3}{11}$

30. 77

31. 0.675

32. 38_{10}.

33. 640

34. 1.

35. 15

36. 19

37. $-40a^2b^2$

38. 32

39. 20

40. 3125

Mathcounts Speed and Accuracy Practice Tests　　　　　　　　　　**Test 5**

Part II:

41. $\frac{21}{10}$.

42. 1.

43. 91.

44. 176.

45. 30°.

46. 76 (%).

47. 18.

48. 1/8.

49. $-3c$.

50. 15.

51. 1/4.

52. 90 (degrees).

53. 58/81.

54. −23.

55. $-\frac{3}{2}$.

56. 96°

57. 0.

58. 20.

59. 22.

60. 12.

61. 40 miles per hour.

62. 176 yards.

63. 7.

64. 5/16.

65. 21/32.

66. 2.

67. 1/125.

68. 2015.

69. 28

70. 1300.

71. 961.

72. 64.

73. 12.

74. $6.75.

75. 35

76. 7 hours.

77. 26.

78. 35.

39. 55.

80. 35.

Mathcounts Speed and Accuracy Practice Tests   Test 5

Solutions to Part II:

41. Solution: $\dfrac{21}{10}$.

$\dfrac{1}{3} + \dfrac{1}{7} = \dfrac{10}{21}$.

The answer is $\dfrac{21}{10}$.

42. Solution: 1.

$\dfrac{a^2}{b} = 1 \quad \Rightarrow \quad a^2 = b \quad \Rightarrow \quad a^2 - b = 0 \quad \Rightarrow \quad a^2 - b + 1 = 1.$

43. Solution: 91.

Let the score on the next test be x.

$92 + 89 + 100 + x = 93 \times 4 \quad \Rightarrow \quad 92 + 89 + 100 + x = 372 - 281 = 91.$

44. Solution: 176.

Lu reads 50 pages in 2: 05 – 1: 25 = 50 minutes. $\dfrac{50}{40} = \dfrac{220}{p} \quad \Rightarrow \quad p = 176.$

45. Solution: 30°.

The new triangle is similar to the original triangle. So its sides changes but not the angles. The smallest angle of the new triangle measures is still 30°.

46. Solution: 76 (%).

$1 - \dfrac{6}{25} = \dfrac{19}{25} = 0.76$.

47. Solution: 18.

Method 1:

We can have at most 4! = 24 different positive four-digit integers.

We take off the integers with "0" as the thousands digit: 3! = 6.

The answer is 24 − 6 = 18.

Method 2:

We have 3 ways to choose the thousands digit, 3 ways to choose the hundreds digit, and 2 ways to choose the units digit. So by fundamental counting principle, the answer is $3 \times 3 \times 2 = 18$.

48. Solution: 1/8.

Let the number be x.

$x \times 9 = x + 1$ $\Rightarrow$ $8x = 1$ $\Rightarrow$ $x = 1/8$.

49. Solution: $-3c$.

$a - x + c = -y + b$ \hfill (1)

$x = y - 2c$ $\Rightarrow$ $x - y = -2c$ \hfill (2)

Re-write (1) as: $a + c = x - y + b$ \hfill (3)

Substituting (2) into (3): $a + c = -2c + b$ $\Rightarrow$ $a - b = -3c$.

50. Solution: 15.

Using the worst case scenario, we take out 4 red balls first. Next we take out 5 yellow balls. Finally we take out 5 black balls. Now we only need to take out one ball to guarantee getting 6 balls of the same color. The answer is $4 + 5 + 5 + 1 = 15$.

51. Solution: 1/4.

There are 25 prime numbers less than 100.

So the probability is $25/100 = 1/4$.

52. Solution: 90 (degrees).

The number of degrees in the smaller angle formed by the hour and minute hands of a clock at 1 p.m. is 90°. The smaller angle formed by the hour and minute hands at 6 p.m. is 180°. The positive difference is 180° − 90° = 90°.

53. Solution: 58/81.

Total we have $9 \times 9 = 81$ small squares.

The white part is $6 \times 9 + 4 = 58$. So the answer is 58/81.

Mathcounts Speed and Accuracy Practice Tests　　　　　　　　　　　　　　　　　**Test 5**

54. Solution: −23.
We know that $(k, -5)$ lies on the line. $k - 4(-5) = -3$　　⇒　　$k = -23$.

55. Solution: $-\dfrac{3}{2}$.

$3x + 2y = 2$　⇒　$2y = -3x + 2$　⇒　$y = -\dfrac{3}{2}x + 2$.

The slope is $-\dfrac{3}{2}$.

56. Solution: 96°

The minute hand moves $\dfrac{360°}{60 \text{ minutes}} = 6°$ per minute.

$22 - 6 = 16$ minutes. So the angle moved is $16 \times 6 = 96°$.

57. Solution: 0.
The remainder is 1 when 13^{13} is divided by 13.
$1 + 5 = 6$.
So the remainder when $13^{13} + 5$ is divided by 6 is 0.

58. Solution: 20.
Let p, c, and e be the weights of each pencil, paper clip, and eraser, respectively.
$p + 7c = 3e$　　　　　　　　　　　　　　　　　(1)
$p = 23c$　　　　　　　　　　　　　　　　　　(2)

Substituting (2) into (1): $30c = 3e$　⇒　$20c = 2e$.
So the answer is 20.

59. Solution: 22.
Let a and b be the lengths of two bases, and h be the height.
$\dfrac{(a+b)h}{2} = 11(a+b)$　　　⇒　　$h = 22$.

Mathcounts Speed and Accuracy Practice Tests — Test 5

60. Solution: 12.
Method 1:
We see that $b < 10$.

$7a + 11b = 100 \Rightarrow 7a + 7b + 4b = 100 \Rightarrow a + b = \dfrac{100 - 4b}{7} = \dfrac{4(25 - b)}{7}$.

Since 4 and 7 are relatively prime, for the integer value of $a + b$, we have $25 - b = 7$, 14, or 21. We know that $b < 10$. Thus $25 - b = 21 \Rightarrow a + b = 12$.

Method 2:
$7a + 11b = 100 \Rightarrow 11b \equiv 2 \mod 7 \Rightarrow 4b \equiv 2 \mod 7$
$\Rightarrow 4b \equiv 2 + 7 + 7 = 16 \mod 7 \Rightarrow b \equiv 4 \mod 7$.
$7a + 11 \times b = 100 \Rightarrow a = 8$.
So $a + b = 8 + 4 = 12$.

61. Solution: 40 miles per hour.

$\dfrac{2}{\dfrac{1}{60} + \dfrac{1}{30}} = 40$.

62. Solution: 176 yards.
By the proportion:
$\dfrac{110}{40} = \dfrac{x}{64} \Rightarrow x = 176$.

63. Solution: 7.
$250 \div 27 = 9 \, r \, 7$.
Seven students received 10 rubber bands than others (received 9).

64. Solution: 5/16.
We will have HHTTT. The number of arrangements will be $\dfrac{5!}{3! \times 2!} = 10$.

The probability is $P = \dfrac{10}{2 \times 2 \times 2 \times 2 \times 2} = \dfrac{5}{16}$.

65. Solution: 21/32.
Let The length of the side of the $ABCD$ be 8.

Mathcounts Speed and Accuracy Practice Tests   **Test 5**

$$\frac{\frac{4 \times 4}{2} \times 2 + 12 + 14}{8 \times 8} = \frac{21}{32}$$

66. Solution: 2.
Let s be the number of stools and c be the number of chairs.
$3s + 4c = 20$ $\Rightarrow$ $3s = 4(5 - c)$.
We know that 3 and 4 are relatively prime. So $s = 4$ and $c = 2$.

67. Solution: 1/125.
Since two models are similar, the ratio of their volumes is $\frac{V_1}{V_2} = (\frac{1}{5})^3 = \frac{1}{125}$

68. Solution: 2015.
Let L be the length and W be the width of the original rectangle.
$LW + 2L + 2W + m = (L + 3)(W + 3)$ $\Rightarrow$ $m = L + W + 9 = 2006 + 9 = 2015$.

69. Solution: 28
Let n be the number of people in the choir.

Method 1:
When they are arranged by 5, the possible number of people is
3, 8, 13, 18, 23, 28, 33, 38, 43, 48, 53, 58, ...
When they are arranged by 6, the possible number of people is
4, 10, 16, 22, 28, 34, 40, 46, 52, 58, ...
The numbers 28 and 58 are all possible answers. The least number is 28.

Method 2:
$n \equiv 3 \quad \text{mod } 5$ (1)
$n \equiv 4 \quad \text{mod } 6$ (2)
$n + 2 \equiv 0 \quad \text{mod } 5$ (3)
$n + 2 \equiv 0 \quad \text{mod } 6$ (4)

So $n + 2 \equiv 0 \quad \text{mod } 30$ (5)
$n = 30 - 2 = 28$.

70. Solution: 1300.

$29 \times 31 + 19 \times 21 + 2 = (30 - 1)(30 + 1) + (20 - 1)(20 + 1) + 2$
$= 30^2 - 1 + 20^2 - 1 + 2 = 1300$.

71. Solution: 961.

We separate 62 into two numbers such that they are as close as possible to get the maximum value of the product: $62 = 31 + 31$.
The product is $31^2 = 961$.

72. Solution: 64.

Applying Pythagorean Theorem to $\triangle XYW$:
$YW^2 = XY^2 - XW^2 = 17^2 - 15^2 = 64$
We also know that $YW^2 = XW \times WZ = 64$

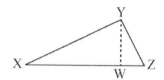

73. Solution: 12.

We can get a sum of 3, 6, 9, and 12.

$3 = 1 + 2$	2 ways.
$6 = 5 + 1 = 4 + 2 = 3 + 3$	5 ways.
$9 = 6 + 3 = 5 + 4$	4 ways.
$12 = 6 + 6$	1 way.

Total 12 ways.

74. Solution: $6.75.

Let n be the number of nickels q be the number of quarters.

$n + q = 39$ (1)
$n + 9 = q$ (2)

Substituting (2) into (1): $2n + 9 = 39 \Rightarrow 2n = 30 \Rightarrow n = 15$
So $q = 24$.
$5n + 25q = 5 \times 15 + 24 \times 25 = 75 + 600 = 675 = \$6.75$

75. Solution: 35

If we use only one color, we have four combinations: rrrr, bbbb, yyyy, wwww.
If we use two colors, say we use three red marbles, we have
rrrw   rrry   rrrb.
Similarly we get $4 \times 3 = 12$ combination.

We have 6 more combinations with two colors:

rrww   rryy   rrbb

wwyy   wwbb

yybb

If we use three colors, say we use two red marbles, we have

rryw   rryb   rrbw

Similarly we get 4 × 3 = 12 combination.

If we use four colors, we have one combination: rbyw.

Total we have 4 + 12 + 6 + 12 + 1 = 35 different combinations.

76. Solution: 7 hours.

$$\frac{65}{35} = \frac{780}{x} \quad\Rightarrow\quad x = \frac{780 \times 35}{65} = 420 \text{ minutes} = 7 \text{ hours}.$$

77. Solution: 26.

Number of edges: 6 × 2 + 6 = 18.

Number of faces: 1 × 2 + 6 = 8.

The answer is 18 + 8 = 26.

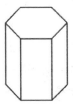

78. Solution: 35.

We factor 306 such that the two factors are as close as possible. 306 = 1 × 302 = 2 × 153 = 3 × 102 = 5 × 51 = 9 × 34 = 17 × 18. The answer is 17 + 18 = 35.

79. Solution: 55.

Any two points will from a chord. $\binom{11}{2} = \frac{11 \times 10}{2} = 55$

80. Solution: 35.

Alex can put 6 red balls in a row. There are seven spaces and then he can put four green balls between these red balls as shown in the figure. The number of ways is

$\binom{7}{4} = \binom{7}{3} = \frac{7 \times 6 \times 5}{3 \times 2 \times 1} = 35$.

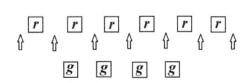

MATHCOUNTS

■ **Speed and Accuracy Practice Test 6**■

Name
_____

Date
_____

DO NOT BEGIN UNTIL YOU ARE INSTRUCTED TO DO SO.
The test consists of two parts, with each part 40 problems. You will have 15 minutes to complete the part 1 and 25 minutes to complete the part 2. You are not allowed to use calculators, books, or any other aids during this round. Calculations may be done on scratch paper. All answers must be complete, legible, and simplified to lowest terms. Record only final answers. Do each problem as quick as you can. If you finish one problem, go to the next. Do not spend any time to check your answers.

	Total Correct	Scorer's Initials
Part I		
Part II		

©www.mymathcounts.com

Mathcounts Speed and Accuracy Practice Test 6

Part I Problems 1–40

Mathcounts Speed and Accuracy Practice Tests — Test 6

1. $2014 + 2016 =$

2. $\dfrac{3}{7} - \dfrac{3}{9} =$

3. $65 \times 25 =$ ———

4. $19 \times 91 =$

5. Express $\dfrac{13}{20}$ as a decimal.

6. 70% of 600 is

7. $725 \times 11 =$

8. $100 \div 2.5 =$ ———

9. Express 2.5×1.9 as a mixed number.

10. $10 \times 9\dfrac{2}{5} =$

11. If a can of 4 tennis balls costs $4.50, then 80 balls cost $ ———

12. $64 \times 66 =$

13. If $\dfrac{x}{3} + 6 = 2$, then $x =$ ———

14. $196 \times 101 =$ ———

15. $\sqrt{841} =$

16. $43 \times 63 =$

17. $17 \times 43 =$

18. $89 \times 91 =$

19. $8\dfrac{2}{3} \div 4\dfrac{2}{3} =$ ——— mixed number

20. Express 33_5 is base 10.

21. $16 \times 0.125 =$

22. $16^2 - 11^2 =$ ———

23. $69^2 \div 4$ has a remainder of ———

24. The prime twin of 101 is———

25. The smallest palindrome greater than 2014 is

Mathcounts Speed and Accuracy Practice Tests — Test 6

26. The difference between the supplement and the complement of a 60° angle is —°

27. Express $\frac{6}{7} + \frac{7}{6}$ as a mixed number.

28. $\sqrt{1\frac{24}{25}} = $ ——

29. 12.5% of 2800 is ——

30. Find the number of elements of $\{1, 2, 3, 4\} \cup \{5, 3, 2\}$.

31. 0.125 mile = —— feet

33. Express $0.\overline{45}$ as a common fraction.

33. What is the 5th triangular number?

34. 6! = ——

35. The probability of drawing a blue marble from a bag that contains 16 red and 10 blue marbles is——

36. The distance between $(0, -37)$ and $(-9, 3)$ is ——

37. The next term of 3, 4, 7, 11, … is

38. If $f(x) = x - 3$, then $-2f(-2) =$

39. $(x - 9)^2 =$

40. Express $1 + 1$ in the binary numeral system.

Mathcounts Speed and Accuracy Practice Test 6

Part II Problems 41–80

Mathcounts Speed and Accuracy Practice Tests   Test 6

41. How many books can Ed buy for $13 each and spend the same amount he would spend to buy 143 books for $7 each?

42. What is the largest prime that is a factor of the sum 6! + 1?

43. What is the value of $6x$ if $3x + 7 = 22$?

44. The sum of the first n odd positive integers is 256. What is the value of n?

45. A bookstore employee is given a 25% discount off the retail price of any book. Assuming there is no tax, how many dollars does she pay for a book with a retail price of $68?

46. If an isosceles triangle has base angles that are each four times the measure of the smaller angle, what is the degree measure of one of the base angles?

47. Tom's math homework is on seven consecutive pages in the math textbook, and the sum of those page numbers is 637. What is the page number of the next page after these five homework pages?

48. The intersection of a circular region of radius 5 inches and a circular region of radius 7 inches has area 5π in². In square inches, what is the area of the total region covered by the two circular regions? Express your answer in terms of π.

49. What is the value of the product 57×63?

50. What is the ratio of the number of degrees in the interior angle of a regular decagon to the number of degrees in the interior angle of a regular dodecagon? Express your answer as a common fraction.

51. Mary buys a different number of 50¢ and 75¢ candy bars and spends $10, not including tax. What is the smallest possible number of 75¢ candy bars could she buy?

52. A restaurant automatically adds an 16% tip to the bill. If the tip was $24, what was the bill before the tip was added, in dollars?

53. The integer 2,019 can be expressed as the sum of two prime numbers in exactly one way. What is the larger of the two primes in this sum?

54. Let x be an integer that satisfies $x^4 - 56 = 200$. What is the value of $x^2 - 4$?

55. Triangle ABC has sides of length 9, 40, and 41 units. What is the mean, in degrees, of the measures of the three angles?

56. The number 25 can be written as the sum of ten consecutive integers. What is the product of these integers?

57. When expressed as a common fraction, what is the value of $\dfrac{3+6+9+...+3021}{2+4+6+...+2014}$?

58. What is the probability that the sum of the digits of a randomly selected two-digit positive integer will be 11? Express your answer as a common fraction.

59. What is the greatest prime factor of the difference $74^2 - 71^2$?

60. The three circles in this figure are all tangent. Their centers are collinear. The diameter of the smallest circle is 1/5 that of the largest circle with the diameter D. What is the shaded area in terms of D? Express your answer as a common fraction.

Mathcounts Speed and Accuracy Practice Tests — Test 6

61. If the five points marked by dots on the number line below are equally spaced, what is the value of 2x?

62. What is the number of square meters in the area of a square if the length of a diagonal is 16 meters?

63. How many miles are traveled driving at 90 mi/h for 90 minutes?

64. When the positive integer x is divided by each of 6, 7 and 8, it has a remainder of 3. What is the sum of the three smallest possible values of x?

65. The sum of the interior angles of a convex polygon is 2700°. How many sides does the polygon have?

66. How many positive integers between 200 and 500 are divisible by 14?

67. What is the least value of n for which a regular n-gon has at least 20 diagonals?

68. What is the value of the difference $2016^2 - 2014^2$?

69. What is the value of the quotient $\dfrac{(1-\frac{1}{2})(1-\frac{1}{2})(1-\frac{1}{2})\cdots(1-\frac{2013}{2014})}{\frac{1}{2015!}}$

70. Alex is 5 years older than Bob. Ten years ago the sum of their ages was 15. In years, how old is Bob now?

71. What is the value of $\sqrt{2015^2 - 2\times 2014 \times 2013 + 2014^2}$?

Mathcounts Speed and Accuracy Practice Tests — Test 6

72. Together three puppies and three adult dogs weigh 75 pounds. Two adult dogs and four puppies have a combined weight of 80 pounds. If each of the puppies has the same weight and each of the adult dogs has the same weight, how many pounds does one puppy weigh?

73. How many distinct factors of 100! are prime numbers?

74. A regular hexagon of side length 2 inches is divided into four triangles by three nonintersecting diagonals. What is the average area, in square inches, of each of the four triangles? Express your answer in simplest radical form.

75. What is the value of x if $\dfrac{\sqrt{3}}{5x} = \dfrac{5}{15 \times \sqrt{12}}$. Express the answer as a common fraction.

76. Sharon bikes 15 mi at 5 mi/h and 5 mi at 15 mi/h. What is Sharon's average speed, in miles per hour, for the whole trip?

77. The three angle measures of a triangle are $\dfrac{x}{5}$, $\dfrac{x}{7}$, and $\dfrac{3x}{35}$ degrees. What is the degree measure of the smallest angle?

78. For how many integers x is $(x-5)(x+4) < 0$?

79. What is the value of $0.\overline{1} + 0.\overline{2} + 0.\overline{3} + 0.\overline{4} + 0.\overline{5} + 0.\overline{6} + 0.\overline{7} + 0.\overline{8} + 0.\overline{9}$?? Express your answer as a common fraction.

80. If one integer is selected randomly from 1 to 100, what is the probability that its reciprocal is a terminating decimal?

Mathcounts Speed and Accuracy Practice Tests Test 6

Answer Keys:

<u>Part I:</u>

1. 4030
2. $\dfrac{2}{21}$
3. 1625
4. 1729
5. 0.65
6. 420
7. 7975
8. 40
9. $4\dfrac{3}{4}$.
10. 94
11. 90
12. 4224
13. −12
14. 19,796

15. 29
16. 2709
17. 731
18. 8099
19. $1\dfrac{6}{7}$
20. 18_{10}
21. 2
22. 135
23. 1
24. 103
25. 2112.
26. 90°.
27. $2\dfrac{1}{42}$

28. $\dfrac{7}{5}$, $1\dfrac{2}{5}$
29. 350
30. 5
31. 660
33. $\dfrac{5}{11}$
33. 15
34. 720
35. $\dfrac{5}{13}$.
36. 41.
37. 18
38. $-2f(-2) = 10$
39. $x^2 - 18x + 81$
40. 10.

Mathcounts Speed and Accuracy Practice Tests — Test 6

Part II:

41. 77.

42. 103

43. 30.

44. 16.

45. $51.

46. 80°.

47. 95.

48. 69π (in²).

49. 3591

50. $\dfrac{24}{25}$.

51. 2.

52. 150.

53. 2017.

54. 12.

55. 60°.

56. 0.

57. 3/2.

58. 4/45.

59. 29.

60. $\dfrac{1}{25}\pi D^2$.

61. 9.

62. 128 m².

63. 135.

64. 1017.

65. 17.

66. 21.

67. 8.

68. 8060.

69. 2015.

70. 15.

71. 1

72. 15

73. 25.

74. $3\sqrt{3}/2$ (in²)

75. 18/5.

76. 6 mi/h.

77. 36 degrees

78. 8.

79. 5.

80. 3/20.

Mathcounts Speed and Accuracy Practice Tests   Test 6

Solutions to Part II:

41. Solution: 77.
Let x be the number of books $13 each.
$x \times 13 = 143 \times 7 \quad \Rightarrow \quad x \times 13 = 11 \times 13 \times 7 \Rightarrow \quad x = 11 \times 7 = 77$,

42. Solution: 103.
$6! + 1 = 720 + 1 = 721 = 7 \times 103$.

43. Solution: 30.
$3x + 7 = 22 \quad \Rightarrow \quad 3x = 15 \quad \Rightarrow \quad 6x = 15 \times 2 = 30$.

44. Solution: 16.
$1 + 3 + 5 + \ldots + n = n^2 \quad \Rightarrow \quad n^2 = 256 = 16^2 \quad \Rightarrow \quad n = 16$.

45. Solution: $51.
$25\% \times \$68 = \$51$.

46. Solution: 80°.
Let the third angle be $x°$.
$4x + 4x + x = 180° \quad \Rightarrow \quad x = 20° \quad \Rightarrow \quad 4x = 80°$.

47. Solution: 95.
$637/7 = 91$. So the fourth page is 91. The next page is the eighth page.
So it is $91 + 1 + 1 + 1 + 1 = 95$.

48. Solution: 69π (in^2).
The total area is $\pi \times 5^2 + \pi \times 7^2 - 5\pi = 69\pi$

49. Solution: 3591
Method 1:
$57 \times 63 = (60 - 3)(60 + 3) = 60^2 - 9 = 3600 - 9 = 3591$.

Method 2:
When the sum of the last digits of two numbers is 10, write the smaller number first: 57×63.
$7 \times 3 + 70 = 91$

Mathcounts Speed and Accuracy Practice Tests   Test 6

$50 \times 60 + 500 = 3500$
$3500 + 91 = 3591$.

50. Solution: $\dfrac{24}{25}$.

A regular decagon has 10 sides. A regular decagon has 12 sides.

The interior angle of a regular polygon is $\dfrac{(n-2) \times 180}{n}$. $\dfrac{\frac{(10-2) \times 180}{10}}{\frac{(12-2) \times 180}{12}} = \dfrac{8 \times 12}{10 \times 10} = \dfrac{24}{25}$.

51. Solution: 2.
Let x and y be the of 50¢ and 75¢ candy bars, respectively.
$50x + 75y = 1000 \Rightarrow 2x + 3y = 40$
The smallest value of y is 2.

52. Solution: 150.
Let x be the bill before the tip was added.
$1.16x = 24 + x \Rightarrow 0.16x = 24 \Rightarrow x = 150$

53. Solution: 2017.
Since 2019 is odd and is the sum of two prime number, one must be 2 and the other one is $2009 - 2 = 2017$.

54. Solution: 12.
$x^4 - 56 = 200 \Rightarrow x^4 = 256 \Rightarrow x^2 = 16 \Rightarrow x^2 - 4 = 12$.

55. Solution: 60°.
The sum of three angles of a triangle is always 180°. The mean, in degrees, of the measures of the three angles is always 60°.

56. Solution: 0.
$1 + 2 + 3 + 4 + 5 + 6 + 7 + 8 + 9 = 45 > 25$.
So we know that there must be some negative numbers. Since these ten numbers are consecutive, from positive to negative, it must be a zero in them. So the product is 0.

57. Solution: 3/2.

Mathcounts Speed and Accuracy Practice Tests　　　　　　　　　　　Test 6

$$\frac{3+6+9+\ldots+3021}{2+4+6+\ldots+2014} = \frac{3(1+2+3+\ldots+1007)}{2(1+2+3+\ldots+1007)} = \frac{3}{2}$$

58. Solution: 4/45.
There are 90 two-digit positive integers.
$9 + 2 = 8 + 3 = 7 + 4 = 6 + 5$.
So we have 8 such numbers. The answer is 8/90 = 4/45.

59. Solution: 29.
$74^2 - 71^2 = (74 - 71)(74 + 71) = 3 \times 145 = 3 \times 5 \times 29$.

60. Solution: $\frac{1}{25}\pi D^2$.
Let d_1 be the diameter of the smallest circle and d_2 be the diameter of the second largest circle.
$d_1 + d_2 = D$　　　　　　　　　　　　　　　　　　(1)
$d_1 = \frac{1}{5}D$　　　　　　　　　　　　　　　　　　(2)

Substituting (2) into (1): $\frac{1}{5}D + d_2 = D$　　$\Rightarrow$　　$d_2 = \frac{4}{5}D$.

The shaded area is

$$\frac{\frac{1}{4}\pi D^2}{2} - \frac{\frac{1}{4}\pi d_1^2 + \frac{1}{4}\pi d_2^2}{2} = \frac{1}{8}\pi(D^2 - d_1^2 - d_1^2) = \frac{1}{8}\pi[D^2 - (\frac{1}{5}D)^2 - (\frac{4}{5}D)^2]$$

$$= \frac{1}{8}\pi(D^2 - \frac{17}{25}D^2) = \frac{1}{8}\pi D^2(1 - \frac{17}{25}) = \frac{1}{25}\pi D^2.$$

61. Solution: 9.
$3 + y = 2x$　　　$\Rightarrow$　　$6 + 2y = 4x$　　　　(1)
$3 + 2x = 2y$　　　　　　　　　　　　　　　　　(2)
(1) + (2): $6 + 2y + 3 + 2x = 2y + 4x$　$\Rightarrow$　　$2x = 9$.

62. Solution: 128 m².
This is a $8\sqrt{2}$-$8\sqrt{2}$-16 right triangle. The area is $8\sqrt{2} \times 8\sqrt{2} = 128$ m².

63. Solution: 135.

Mathcounts Speed and Accuracy Practice Tests   Test 6

$$\frac{90 \text{ miles}}{60 \text{ minutes}} = \frac{x \text{ miles}}{90 \text{ minutes}} \quad \Rightarrow \quad x = 135 \text{ miles.}$$

64. Solution: 1017.
The least common multiple of 6, 7, and 8 is 168. The smallest positive integer is $168 + 3 = 171$. The following two numbers are $171 + 168$, and $172 + 168 + 168$. The sum is $168 \times 3 + 171 \times 3 = 3(168 + 171) = 1017$.

65. Solution: 17.
$(n - 2) \times 180 = 2700 \quad \Rightarrow \quad n - 2 = 15 \quad \Rightarrow \quad n = 17.$

66. Solution: 21.
$\left\lfloor \frac{500}{14} \right\rfloor - \left\lfloor \frac{200}{14} \right\rfloor = 35 - 14 = 21$.

67. Solution: 8.
$\binom{n}{2} - n = 20 \quad \Rightarrow \quad \frac{n(n-1)}{2} - n = 20 \quad \Rightarrow \quad \frac{n^2 - n - 2n}{2} = 20 \quad \Rightarrow$
$n^2 - 3n = 40 \quad \Rightarrow \quad n(n-3) = 40 \quad \Rightarrow \quad n = 8.$

68. Solution: 8060.
$2016^2 - 2014^2 = (2016 - 2014)(2016 + 2014) = 2 \times 4030 = 8060.$

69. Solution: 2015.
$$\frac{(1-\frac{1}{2})(1-\frac{1}{2})(1-\frac{1}{2})\cdots(1-\frac{2013}{2014})}{\frac{1}{2015!}} = \frac{\frac{1}{2} \cdot \frac{1}{3} \cdot \frac{1}{4} \cdots \frac{1}{2014}}{\frac{1}{2015!}} = \frac{\frac{1}{2014!}}{\frac{1}{2015!}} = \frac{2015!}{2014!} = 2015$$

70. Solution: 15.
$j - b = 5$ (1)
$j - 10 + b - 10 = 15 \quad \Rightarrow \quad j + b = 35$ (2)
(2) − (1): $b = 15.$

71. Solution: 1
$\sqrt{2015^2 - 2 \times 2015 \times 2016 + 2016^2} = \sqrt{(2015 - 2016)^2} = 1$

72. Solution: 15

$3p + 3a = 75$ $\Rightarrow$ $p + a = 25$ (2)
$4p + 2a = 80$ $\Rightarrow$ $2p + a = 40$ (2)

(2) − (1): $p = 15$.

73. Solution: 25.
There are 25 prime numbers less than 100.

74. Solution: $3\sqrt{3}/2$ (in^2)

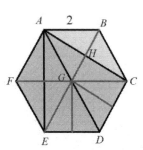

The average area is 3 × the area of triangle *ABH*. Triangle *ABH* is a 30-60-90 right triangle with the side lengths 1, $\sqrt{3}$, 2 and the area $\sqrt{3}/2$.
So the answer is $3\sqrt{3}/2$.

75. Solution: 18/5.

$$\frac{\sqrt{3}}{5x} = \frac{5}{15 \times \sqrt{12}} \Rightarrow \frac{\sqrt{3}}{5x} = \frac{1}{3 \times 2\sqrt{3}} \Rightarrow 5x = 18 \Rightarrow x = \frac{18}{5}.$$

76. Solution: 6 mi/h.

$$v = \frac{d}{t} = \frac{15 + 5}{\frac{15}{5} + \frac{5}{15}} = 6.$$

77. Solution: 36 degrees

$$\frac{x}{5} + \frac{x}{7} + \frac{3x}{35} = 180° \Rightarrow \frac{15x}{35} = 180° \Rightarrow x = 420°$$

$$\frac{3x}{35} = 36.$$

78. Solution: 8.
We get 8 integers from -3 to 4.

79. Solution: 5.
$0.\overline{1} + 0.\overline{2} + 0.\overline{3} + 0.\overline{4} + 0.\overline{5} + 0.\overline{6} + 0.\overline{7} + 0.\overline{8} + 0.\overline{9}$

$$=\frac{1}{9}+\frac{2}{9}+\frac{3}{9}+\frac{4}{9}+\frac{5}{9}+\frac{6}{9}+\frac{7}{9}+\frac{8}{9}+\frac{9}{9}=\frac{45}{9}=5.$$

80. Solution: 3/20.

If the denominator has only 2 and 5 as its factors, this fraction can become a terminating decimal. The length of the decimal part equals the greater power of 2 or 5.

The reciprocals of numbers can be a terminating decimal:

2	4	8	16	32	64
5	25				
10	20	40	80		
50					
1	100				

$P = 15/100 = 3/20$.

MATHCOUNTS

■ Speed and Accuracy Practice Test 7■

Name

Date

DO NOT BEGIN UNTIL YOU ARE INSTRUCTED TO DO SO.
The test consists of two parts, with each part 40 problems. You will have 15 minutes to complete the part 1 and 25 minutes to complete the part 2. You are not allowed to use calculators, books, or any other aids during this round. Calculations may be done on scratch paper. All answers must be complete, legible, and simplified to lowest terms. Record only final answers. Do each problem as quick as you can. If you finish one problem, go to the next. Do not spend any time to check your answers.

	Total Correct	Scorer's Initials
Part I		
Part II		

©www.mymathcounts.com

Mathcounts Speed and Accuracy Practice Test 7

Part I Problems 1–40

Mathcounts Speed and Accuracy Practice Tests Test 7

1. What is $1024^{0.1}$?

2. Express 96% as a fraction in the simplest form.

3. $31 \times 65 =$

4. $187 \div 17 =$

5. $(8 \times 1000) + (8 \times 100) + (8 \times 10) + 8 \times 1 =$

6. $838 - 383 =$

7. Find the remainder when 5,937 is divided by 4.

8. $\dfrac{7}{9} - \dfrac{1}{3} = \left(\dfrac{x}{y}\right)^2$. Find smallest possible value of $x + y$.

9. Is it true that $\dfrac{6}{13} > \dfrac{4}{9}$?

10. $4.5 \times 28 =$

11. 36 inches = ―― feet

12. $(-22) + (-8) \times (-4) =$

13. $11 \div 0.25 =$

14. $55 \times 55 =$

15. If $7a - 4 = 3a + 32$, then $a =$

16. The GCF of 58 and 174 is

17. $12.5 \times 8 =$

18. $24 \times 16 - 24 - 16 =$

19. $7\dfrac{4}{13} \times 7\dfrac{7}{13} =$ ―― mixed number

20. MMXV = ―― Arabic number

21. The number of positive, proper fractions in lowest terms with denominator 13 is ――

22. $13 \times 9\dfrac{7}{13} =$

23. 7 is 35% of what number?

24. $\sqrt{1521} =$

25. $\dfrac{1}{12}$ miles = ―― in

26. If $f(x) = x^2 - 50$, then $f(10) =$

27. Find the number of odd subsets of the set (ω, β, π, Δ).

28. Subtracting 31% of a number from the number is the same as multiplying the number by — %.

29. The geometric mean between 25 and 16 is —

30. The slope of the line passing through (0, 0) and (1, −3) is

31. 60 miles/hour = —— feet/sec

32. $7! \div 4! =$

33. The product of the GCF and the LCM of 11 and 45 is

34. If the hypotenuse of a 45-45-90 triangle measures $13\sqrt{2}$, then a leg measures —

35. The surface area of a cube with edge $\sqrt{15}$ is

36. 100 feet = —— cm

37. $\dfrac{13}{16} \times \dfrac{32}{26} =$ ——

38. 42 is —— % less than 60

39. $\binom{10}{0} + \binom{10}{1} + \binom{10}{2} + \binom{10}{3} + \binom{10}{4} + \binom{10}{5}$
$+ \binom{10}{6} + \binom{10}{7} + \binom{10}{8} + \binom{10}{9} + \binom{10}{10} =$

40. What is the value of $9 \times 9 - 9 + 9 \div 9$?

Mathcounts Speed and Accuracy Practice Test 7

Part II Problems 41–80

41. Four couples went to the movies together. They all sit in eight adjacent seats in the same row. How many different ways can they be seated if each couple sits together?

42. Express 0.5_{10} in base 2.

43. What is the product of the least common multiple and the greatest common factor of 24 and 48?

44. Alex has twice as many cookies as Bob and half as many cookies as Cathy. If Bob and Cathy have 40 cookies together, how many cookies does Alex have?

45. Express $0.5^{0.5}$ in the simplest radical form.

46. What is the least of three prime numbers whose product is 2431?

47. The cost of daily school lunch increased from $2.25 to $1.80. What was the percent decrease?

48. When expressed as an integer, what are the last three digits of 2015!?

49. For what value of n is the sum of the first n positive integers equal to 210?

50. An isosceles triangle with sides of integer length has a perimeter of 40 inches. If the ratio of two of its sides is 2:3, what is the greatest possible value in inches in the length of one of the legs?

Mathcounts Speed and Accuracy Practice Tests Test 7

51. A conical pool takes 4 hours to be filled at a uniform rate to a depth of 12 ft. How many minutes does it take to fill it to a depth of 6 ft?

52. For how many integers x is $(x + 4)(x - 5) < 0$?

53. How many diagonals can be drawn in a cube?

54. Eduardo is writing natural numbers. He writes one 1, two 2's, three 3's, and so on: 1, 2, 2, 3, 3, 3, 4, 4, ,4, 4, 5,…. What number is the 100th term?

55. What is the 100th term of the sequence 1, 2, 5, 10, 17, $\cdots$?

56. Richard is thinking of two distinct, positive integers. He tells Barbara their sum is 20, and he tells Lori that their product is 91. What is the sum of the squares of Richard's two numbers?

57. Two sides of a triangle measure 12 units and 19 units. In units, what is the positive difference between the measures of the smallest and the largest possible integral lengths of the third side of the triangle?

58. What is the sum of all positive integers from 1 to 100, inclusive, that are neither multiples of 2 nor perfect squares?

59. Mike has eight U.S. coins with a total value of 62 cents. He does not have any half-dollars. What is the smallest number of dimes does Mike have?

60. The domain of a function $f(x)$ is all real numbers and the range of $f(x)$ is all real numbers from -11 to 11, inclusive. What is the maximum value of $g(x)$ if $g(x) = 11f(x - 11) + 11$?

61. In an arithmetic progression the first term is 0 and the fifth term is 7. What is the third term? Express your answer as a common fraction.

62. The positive real numbers w, x and y satisfy the equation $\dfrac{x}{5} = 20yw^2$. If y is tripled and w is halved, by what percent must x be decreased so that the new values of w, x and y also satisfy the equation?

63. A solid consisting of 15 unit cues placed on a table as shown in the figure is painted from five directions (the bottom is not painted) and is then separated into 15 unit cubes. One unit cube is randomly selected and rolled. What is the probability that the face showing is painted? Express your answer as a fraction.

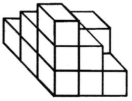

64. How many ways are there to select 3 boys and 2 girls from 6 boys and 4 girls to do 5 different jobs?

65. How many sides does a regular polygon have if the measure of an interior angle is 160 degrees?

66. If $g(x) = 2x - 4$ and $f(x) = 3x^2 + 15x$, what is $f(g(3))$?

67. When all two-digit positive integers are written, what fraction of the digits written are 5's? Express your answer as a common fraction.

Mathcounts Speed and Accuracy Practice Tests   Test 7

68. A bus can hold a maximum of 41 students. What is the minimum number of buses needed to transport 821 students?

69. The product of two consecutive odd whole numbers is 255. What is the smaller number?

70. Set A contains 25 elements, set B contains 22 elements, and the intersection of the sets contains 18 elements. How many elements are in the union of the sets?

71. Find the last four digits of 5^{2014}.

72. Find the remainder when $66^{2015} + 12^{2015}$ is divided by 13.

73. What is the units digit of the base-6 representation of the base-10 number 2015^{2015}?

74. It takes Bryan one hour to dig a hole that is 2.4 meters wide, 3.5 meters long and 1.5 meters deep. At the same rate, how many hours will it take Bryan to dig a hole that is 4.8 meters wide, 10.5 meters long and 3.0 meters deep?

75. From a group of five boys and three girls, two children are selected at random. What is the probability that the second child selected is a girl? Express your answer as a common fraction.

76. The area of triangle ABC is 72 square meters. Point D is on AB such that $BD = 2AD$. Point E is on CD such that $DE = 2EC$. What is the number of square meters in the area of the triangle BCE?

77. What is the value of $13^3 - 9 \times 13^2 + 27 \times 13 - 27$?

78. The price of a IPod was discounted 30% on the first day of a sale. The sale price was then discounted an additional 30% on the second day. What percent is the combined discount?

79. What day of the week will it be 2015 days from Tuesday?

80. There are nine points on the circumference of a circle. All line segments are drawn by connecting two of these 9 points. How many triangles are there if no three line segments go through the same point? The vertices of any triangle must be inside the circle.

Mathcounts Speed and Accuracy Practice Tests Test 7

Answer Keys:

Part I:

1. 2.
2. $\frac{24}{25}$.
3. 2015.
4. 11
5. 8888.
6. 455
7. 1
8. $x + y = 5$.
9. Yes.
10. 126.
11. 3.
12. 10
13. 44
14. 3025
15. $a = 9$
16. 58
17. 100.
18. 344.
19. $55\frac{15}{169}$
20. 2015
21. 12.
22. 124
23. 20
24. 39.
25. 5280.
26. 50
27. 8.
28. 69.
29. 20
30. −3.
31. 88
32. 210
33. 495.
34. 13
35. 90.
36. 3048.
37. 1.
38. 30
39. 1024.
40. 73.

Mathcounts Speed and Accuracy Practice Tests — Test 7

Part II:

41. 384 (ways)

42. 0.1.

43. 1152.

44. 16 (cookies).

45. $\dfrac{\sqrt{2}}{2}$.

46. 11.

47. 20 (percent).

48. 000.

50. 15 (inches).

51. 30 (minutes).

52. 8 (integers).

53. 16 (diagonals).

54. 14.

55. 9802.

56. 218.

57. 23 (units).

58. 2335.

59. 2 (dimes).

60. 132.

61. 7/2.

62. 25%.

63. 7/18.

64. 14400.

65. 18.

66. 42.

67. 19/180.

68. 21.

69. 15.

70. 29.

71. 5625.

72. 0.

73. 5.

74. 12 hours.

75. $\dfrac{3}{8}$.

76. 16 m^2.

77. 1000.

78. 51%.

79. Monday.

80. Solution: 84.

Mathcounts Speed and Accuracy Practice Tests   Test 7

Solutions to Part II:

41. Solution: 384 (ways)
We have four couples so we have 4! = 24 ways to seat them if we think that each couple is a unit. The couple can switch their positions so we have 2^4 = 16 ways of position change. The answer is 24 × 16 = 384.

42. Solution: 0.1.
Begin with the decimal fraction and multiply by 2: $0.5 \times 2 = 1$.
The whole number part of the result is the first binary digit to the right of the point. So the answer is 0.1.

43. Solution: 1152.
LCM (24, 48) × GCF (24, 48) = 24 × 48 = 1152.

44. Solution: 16 (cookies).

$A = 2B \quad \Rightarrow \quad B = \dfrac{1}{2}A \quad\quad\quad (1)$

$A = \dfrac{1}{2}C \quad \Rightarrow \quad C = 2A \quad\quad\quad (2)$

$B + C = 40 \quad\quad\quad (3)$

Substituting (1) and (2) into (3): $\dfrac{1}{2}A + 2A = 40 \quad \Rightarrow \quad \dfrac{5}{2}A = 40 \quad \Rightarrow \quad A = 16$.

45. Solution: $\dfrac{\sqrt{2}}{2}$.

$0.5^{0.5} = \left(\dfrac{1}{2}\right)^{\frac{1}{2}} = \sqrt{\dfrac{1}{2}} = \dfrac{\sqrt{2}}{2}$.

46. Solution: 11.
Since 2 + 3 − (4 + 1) = 0, 2431 is divisible by 11. 2431 = 11 × 221.
Since 22 − 9 × 1 = 13, 221 is divisible by 13. 2431 = 11 × 13 × 17. The answer is 11.

47. Solution: 20 (percent).

$$\frac{2.25-1.80}{2.25}=\frac{0.45}{2.25}=\frac{45}{225}=\frac{1}{5}=20\%.$$

48. Solution: 000.
$2015! = 2015 \times \cdots \times 1000 \times \cdots \times 1$. The last three digits are 000.

49. Solution: 20.
$$\frac{(1+n)n}{2}=210 \quad \Rightarrow \quad (1+n)n = 210 \times 2 = 20 \times 21.$$
So $n = 20$.

50. Solution: 15 (inches).
Since we want the greatest value for the legs, we let the length of one leg be $3x$.
We have $3x + 3x + 2x = 40 \quad \Rightarrow \quad x = 5 \quad \Rightarrow 3x = 15$.

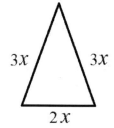

51. Solution: 30 (minutes).
Let V_1 be the conic pool with the depth of 6 ft, V be the conic pool with the depth of 12 ft. t_1 be the time needed fill it to a depth of 3 ft.
$$\frac{t_1}{240}=\frac{V_1}{V}=(\frac{\frac{1}{2}r}{r})^3 \quad \Rightarrow \quad t_1 = 180 \times (\frac{\frac{1}{2}r}{r})^3 = 240 \times \frac{1}{8} = 30.$$

52. Solution: 8 (integers).
x can be $-3, -2, -1, 0, 1, 2, 3$, and 4. Total 8 integers.

53. Solution: 16 (diagonals).
A cube has 8 vertices. At most we can have $\binom{8}{2}=\frac{8\times 7}{2}=28$ diagonals. Since a cube has 12 sides, the answer is $28 - 12 = 16$.

54. Solution: 14.

Mathcounts Speed and Accuracy Practice Tests Test 7

If we group these numbers like this: (1), (2, 2), (3, 3, 3), (4, 4, 4, 4),…, we will get $1 + 2 + \ldots + n = \dfrac{(1+n)n}{2}$ integers from group 1 to group n.

Let the 100th term be in the group n. So $\dfrac{(1+n)n}{2} \geq 100$ $\Rightarrow$ $n(n+1) \geq 200$.

We see that $14 \times 15 = 210$, and $13 \times 14 = 182$. So $n = 14$. In group 14, every integer will be 14. So the 100th term is 14.

55. Solution: 9802.

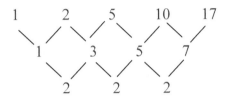

By the Newton's Little Formula:

$$a_n = A\binom{n-1}{0} + B\binom{n-1}{1} + C\binom{n-1}{2} + \cdots\cdots + K\binom{n-1}{m}$$

$$a_{100} = 1 \times \binom{99}{0} + 1 \times \binom{99}{1} + 2 \times \binom{99}{2} = 1 + 99 + 2 \times \dfrac{99 \times 98}{2} = 100 + 9702 = 9802$$

56. Solution: 218.
Let two numbers be x and y.
$x + y = 20$ (1)
$xy = 91$ (2)
Squaring both sides of 1): $(x+y)^2 = 20^2$ $\Rightarrow$ $x^2 + y^2 + 2xy = 20^2$ (3)
Substituting (2) into (3): $x^2 + y^2 + 2 \times 91 = 20^2$ $\Rightarrow$ $x^2 + y^2 = 20^2 - 2 \times 91 = 218$.

57. Solution: 23 (units).
Let x be the possible integral lengths of the third side of the triangle.
By the Triangle Inequality Theorem, $19 - 12 < x < 19 + 12$ $\Rightarrow$ $7 < x < 31$.
The possible values of x is from 8 to 30, inclusive. The answer is $30 - 8 + 1 = 23$.

58. Solution: 2335.

121

Mathcounts Speed and Accuracy Practice Tests   Test 7

$(1 + 3 + 5 + \cdots + 99) - (1^2 + 3^2 + 5^2 + 7^2 + 9^2) = \dfrac{(1+99) \times 50}{2} - 5^2 - (1^2 + 7^2) - (3^2 + 9^2)$
$= 2500 - 25 - 50 - 90 = 2335$.

59. Solution: 2 (dimes).
The following coins will do: 25, 10, 10, 5, 5, 5, 1, 1 or 10, 10, 10, 10, 10, 10, 1, 1. The answer is 2.

60. Solution: 132.
The greatest value for $f(x)$ is 11.
The maximum value of $g(x)$ is achieved when the maximum value of $f(x)$ is achieved. So the maximum value of $g(x)$ is $11 \times 11 + 11 = 11 \times 12 = 132$.

61. Solution: 7/2.
$a_1 + a_5 = 2a_3 \implies a_3 \dfrac{a_1 + a_5}{2} = \dfrac{0 + 7}{2} = \dfrac{7}{2}$.

62. Solution: 25%.

$\dfrac{x}{5} = 20yw^2 \implies x = 100yw^2$ (1)

$\dfrac{mx}{5} = 20(3y)(\dfrac{w}{2})^2 \implies$ (2)

Substituting (1) into (2): $\implies \dfrac{m \times 100yw^2}{5} = 20(3y)(\dfrac{w}{2})^2$

$\implies m \times 100yw^2 = 100 \times 3y \times \dfrac{w^2}{4} \implies m = \dfrac{3}{4} = 75\%$.

So x be decreased by $1 - 75\% = 25\%$.

63. Solution: 7/18.
There are $(7 + 6) \times 2 + 9 = 35$ painted faces all of which are equally likely. There are $15 \times 6 = 90$ faces altogether. Therefore the probability is $35/90 = 7/18$.

64. Solution: 14400.
We have $\binom{6}{3}$ ways to select 3 boys and $\binom{4}{2}$ ways to select 2 girls. Then we have 5!
Ways to assign them 5 different jobs. So the answer is $\binom{6}{3} \times \binom{4}{2} \times 5! = 14400$.

65. Solution: 18.
$$\frac{(n-2)\times 180}{n}=160 \quad \Rightarrow \quad (n-2)\times 9 = 8n \quad \Rightarrow \quad n=18.$$

66. Solution: 42.
$g(x) = 2x - 4 \quad \Rightarrow \quad g(3) = 2 \times 3 - 4 = 2.$
$f(g(3)) = f(2) = 3 \times 2^2 + 15 \times 2 = 12 + 30 = 42.$

67. Solution: 19/180.
Method 1:
We have $9 \times 10 = 90$ two digit positive integers with $90 \times 2 = 180$ digits.
We have eleven 5's in these numbers: 5, 15, 25, 35, 45, 55, 65, 75, 85, 95.
When we switch the digits of 15, 25, 35, 45, 65, 75, 85, 95, we get eight more 5's. The answer is (11 + 8)/180 = 19/180.
Method 2:
We have $9 \times 10 = 90$ two-digit positive integers with $90 \times 2 = 180$ digits.
We have $8 \times 9 = 72$ two-digit positive integers with $72 \times 2 = 144$ digits.
$180 - 144 = 36$. These 36 digits contain $36/2 + 1 = 19$ 5's. So the answer is 19/180.

68. Solution: 21.
$821 \div 41 = 20 \text{ r } 1.$
The minimum number of buses needed to transport 411 students is 21.

69. Solution: 15.
$255 = 5 \times 51 = 5 \times 3 \times 17 = 15 \times 17.$
The answer is 15.

70. Solution: 29.
By the Venn diagram, the answer is $25 + 22 - 18 = 29$.

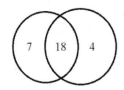

71. Solution: 5625.
$5^5 = 3125$
$5^6 = 5625$
$5^7 = 8125$
$5^8 = 0625$
$5^9 = 3125$
$2014 \quad \Rightarrow \quad 2010 \quad = 4 \times 502 + 2$
The last four digits of 5^{2014} is the same as the last four digits of 5^6. So the answer is 625.

Mathcounts Speed and Accuracy Practice Tests   Test 7

72. Solution: 0.
$66^{2015} + 12^{2015} = (13 \times 5 + 1)^{2015} + (13 - 1)^{2015}$.
The remainder is 1 when $(13 \times 5 + 1)^{2015}$ is divided by 13.
The remainder is -1 or 12 when $(13 - 1)^{2015}$ is divided by 13.
So the remainder is $1 + 12 = 13 \equiv 0$.

73. Solution: 5.
$2015^{2015} \equiv (335 \times 6 + 5)^{2015} \equiv 5^{2015} \equiv (-1)^{2015} \equiv -1 \equiv 5 \pmod{6}$

74. Solution: 12 hours.
Let t be the number of hours needed.
$$\frac{2.4 \times 3.5 \times 1.5}{1} = \frac{4.8 \times 10.5 \times 3.0}{t} \quad \Rightarrow \quad t = 12 \text{ hours.}$$

75. Solution: $\frac{3}{8}$.
Case 1: The first child selected is a boy and the second child selected is a girl.
$P_1 = \frac{5}{8} \times \frac{3}{7} = \frac{15}{56}$

Case 2: The first child selected is a girl and the second child selected is a girl.
$P_2 = \frac{3}{8} \times \frac{2}{7} = \frac{6}{56}$.

The answer is $P = P_1 + P_2 = \frac{15}{56} + \frac{6}{56} = \frac{21}{56} = \frac{3}{8}$.

76. Solution: $16\ m^2$.
$S_{\triangle BCD} = \frac{2}{3} \times 72 = 48$.
$S_{\triangle BCE} = \frac{1}{3} \times S_{\triangle BCD} = \frac{1}{3} \times 48 = 16$.

77. Solution: 1000.
$13^3 - 9 \times 13^2 + 27 \times 13 - 27 = 13^3 + 3 \times 13^2 \times (-3) + 3 \times 13 \times (-3)^2 - 3^3$
$= (13 - 3)^3 = 1000$.

78. Solution: 51%.
Let the original price be x. You still need to pay $70\% \times 70\% \times x = 49\% \times x$.
So the discount is $1 - 49\% = 51\%$.

79. Solution: Monday.
$2015 = 7 \times 287 + 6$.
So the day after 2015 days is the same as the day after 6 days. Six days from Tuesday is Monday.

80. Solution: 84.
As shown in the figure, we need 6 points on the circle to form a triangle with three vertices inside the circle.
The answer is then $\binom{9}{6} = \binom{9}{3} = \frac{9 \times 8 \times 7}{3 \times 2 \times 1} = 84$

MATHCOUNTS

■ **Speed and Accuracy Practice Test 8**■

Name

Date

DO NOT BEGIN UNTIL YOU ARE INSTRUCTED TO DO SO.
The test consists of two parts. Each part has 40 problems. You will have 15 minutes to complete the part 1 and 25 minutes to complete the part 2. You are not allowed to use calculators, books, or any other aids during this round. Calculations may be done on scratch paper. All answers must be complete, legible, and simplified to lowest terms. Record only final answers. Do each problem as quick as you can. If you finish one problem, go to the next. Do not spend any time to check your answers.

	Total Correct	Scorer's Initials
Part I		
Part II		

©www.mymathcounts.com

Mathcounts Speed and Accuracy Practice Test 8

Part I Problems 1–40

Mathcounts Speed and Accuracy Practice Tests — Test 8

1. $6 \times 0.45 =$

2. $\dfrac{3}{4} + \dfrac{2}{4} + \dfrac{3}{4} =$

3. Express 8.5% as a decimal

4. $815 \times 11 =$

5. $3{,}972 - 1{,}746 + 28 - 254 =$

6. $23 \times 17 =$

7. Express the median of 28, 21, 10 and 32 as a fraction.

8. 29 quarters minus 8 dimes = $____

9. $105^2 =$

10. Find the largest prime factor of 1633.

11. Express base 10 numeral 0.8 in base 5.

12. Express $33\dfrac{1}{3}\%$ as a repeating decimal.

13. The perimeter of a rectangle with area 30 and length 6 is

14. Find the remainder of $(92 - 29) \div 7$.

15. $43^2 - 23^2 =$

16. $96 \times 32 =$

17. If $\dfrac{5x}{11} = \dfrac{5}{11x}$, what is the smallest value for x?

18. The radius of a circle with circumference 11π is

19. $7^3 + 3^3 =$

20. $\sqrt{20499} =$

21. 16% of 24 is 64% of

22. $-29^2 =$

23. The sum of the supplement and the compliment of a 30° angle is ___°.

24. 35 is two and one-third of what number?

25. $16 \times 142 =$

Mathcounts Speed and Accuracy Practice Tests   Test 8

26. Express $\frac{21}{40}$ in a percent form ———

27. If $43_b = 39_{10}$, then $b =$ 9

28. $33\frac{1}{3} \times 96 =$

29. $353 \times 101 =$

30. $7\frac{5}{7} \times 483 =$

31. Write $\frac{5}{11} + \frac{11}{5}$ as a mixed number.

32. What is the remainder when $6\frac{1}{3} \times 9\frac{1}{3}$ is divided by 8 ?

33. Express 21_3 in base 5.

34. $7^2 + 24^2 =$

35. 69% of what number is 69?

36. The slope of the line $\frac{1}{4}y = 256x + 17$ is

37. The sum of the roots of the quadratic equation $x^2 + 6x - 9 = 0$ is

38. Expand $(m - 7)^2 =$

39. $72_9 - 54_9 =$ ———

40. $8^2 \times 2^4 =$

Mathcounts Speed and Accuracy Practice Test 8

Part II Problems 41–80

Mathcounts Speed and Accuracy Practice Tests   Test 8

41. What is the sum of the number of faces, vertices and edges in a cube?

42. One-third of a 30-student class is absent today. One-half of the class were absent yesterday. At most how many students are absent in two consecutive days?

43. Compute: $(16+10)^2 - (16-10)^2$.

44. Two of Mr. Smith's classes took the same test. His class of 24 students had an average score of 90. His other class of 36 students had an average of 80. What was the average score for all 60 students?

45. The radius of a circle is increased by 300%. By what percent is the area of the circle increased?

46. Compute $(17 - \sqrt{17^2 - 8^2})^{10}$.

47. What is the least common multiple of 21, 28 and 56?

48. In any given year, the dates (represented as month/day) 4/4, 6/6, 8/8, 10/10 and 12/12 all fall on the same day of the week. April 3, 2015 is a Friday. What day of the week is December 15, 2015?

49. Taylor wants to buy cases to hold her 437 compact discs. Each case holds less than 20 discs. At least how many cases does she need to buy?

50. A board whose length is 144 inches is cut into three pieces in the ratio 3:4:5. What is the number of inches in the length of the longest piece?

51. How many integers can be represented as a difference of two distinct members of the set {1, 2, 3, 4}?

52. At what time is the sum of the digits which represent the hours and minutes on a 12-hour digital watch the greatest?

53. What is the sum of the coordinates of the midpoint of the segment with endpoints (5, 12) and (–7, –2)?

54. A penny *A* is rolling around a second penny *B* without slipping until it returns to its starting point. How many revolutions does *penny A* make?

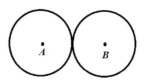

55. What is the sum of all the prime numbers less than 50?

56. Eighteen is 60% of what number?

57. Mike has 88 cents with seven coins. He has no any half-dollars. Find the number of dimes Mike has.

58. What is the number of square units in the area of a triangle whose sides are 9, 40 and 41 units?

59. The point A(–8, 5) is reflected across the *x*-axis onto point B. Point B is reflected over the y-axis onto point C. What is the sum of the coordinates of point C?

60. If $x = 5$ and $y = 4$, then what is the value of $\dfrac{5x^2 - 4y^2}{61}$

61. What is the value of $512 \times 256 \times 128 \times 64 \times \dfrac{1}{2} \times \dfrac{1}{4} \times \dfrac{1}{8} \times \dfrac{1}{16} \times \dfrac{1}{32} \times \dfrac{1}{1024}$?

Mathcounts Speed and Accuracy Practice Tests Test 8

62. Set A has 26 elements and set B has 47 elements. The union of sets A and B has 53 elements. How many elements are in the intersection of sets A and B?

63. John drove at an average rate of 48 miles per hour. How many minutes did it take for him to drive 68 miles?

64. For what value of n does $\dfrac{\sqrt{3} \times \sqrt[3]{3^5}}{3^3} = 3^n$? Express your answer as a common fraction.

65. What part of 10 hours is 10 seconds? Express your answer as a common fraction.

66. The cost of the daily school lunch increased from $1.25 to $1.95. What was the percent increase?

67. For class president, Tim received 45% of the votes, James received 40% of the votes and Anna received the remaining 78 votes. How many votes did Tim receive?

68. Compute: (4 + 14 + 24 + 34) + (96 + 86 + 76 + 66).

69. The average of nine consecutive integers is 23. What is the sum of the least and greatest of these integers?

70. If the sides of a triangle are quadrupled, then the new area is what percent of the original area?

71. Ervin made 32.5% of the shots he took during his basketball game. If he took exactly 40 shots during the game, how many shots did he make?

72. The numbers 1 through 990, inclusive, are printed on a piece of paper. How many digits are printed on the paper?

Mathcounts Speed and Accuracy Practice Tests　　　　　　　　　　　　Test 8

73. How many pairs of prime numbers have a sum of 48?

74. What is the sum of the first 60 positive odd integers?

75. What is the greatest real number that is at least as large as its square minus 6?

76. If the 7th day of the month is on a Tuesday, o what day is the 25th day?

77. It is now 9:45. What time will it be 2 hours 15 minutes?

78. If $2^{2016} - 2^{2015} = 2^x$, what is the value of x?

79. Calculate: $\frac{1}{2} + \frac{1}{4} + \frac{1}{8} + \frac{1}{16} + \frac{1}{32} + \frac{1}{64}$.

80. How many times in a 24 hour period do the hour and minute hands of a clock form a right angle?

Mathcounts Speed and Accuracy Practice Tests Test 8

Answer Keys:

PART I

1. 2.7
2. 2
3. 0.085
4. 8965
5. 2000
6. 391
7. $\dfrac{49}{2}$
8. $6.45
9. 11025
10. 71
11. 0.4.
12. $0.\overline{3}$.
13. 22
14. 0
15. 1320
16. 3072
17. −1.
18. $\dfrac{11}{2}, 5\dfrac{1}{2}, 5.5$
19. 370.
20. 143
21. 6
22. −841
23. 210°.
24. 15
25. 2272
26. 52.5%
27. 9
28. 3200
29. 35653
30. 3726.
31. $2\dfrac{36}{55}$
32. 4
33. 12_5
34. 625
35. 100.
36. 1024.
37. −9
38. $m^2 - 14m + 49$
39. 17_9
40. 1024.

Mathcounts Speed and Accuracy Practice Tests — Test 8

PART II

41. 26.

42. 10.

43. 640.

44. 84.

45. 800%.

46. 1024.

47. 168.

48. Tuesday.

49. 23.

50. 60 inches.

51. 6.

52. 9:59.

53. 4.

54. Two revolutions.

55. 328.

56. 30.

57. 1.

58. 180.

59. 3.

60. 1.

61. 32.

62. 20.

63. 85 minutes.

64. $-5/6$.

65. 1/3600.

66. 56%.

67. 234.

68. 400.

69. 46.

70. 1600 %.

71. 13.

72. 2862.

73. 5 pairs.

74. 3600.

75. 3.

76. Saturday.

77. 12:00.

78. 2015.

79. 63/64.

80. 44.

Mathcounts Speed and Accuracy Practice Tests   **Test 8**

Solutions to Part II:

41. Solution: 26.
A cube has 6 faces, 8 vertices, and 12 edges. The sum is 26.

42. Solution: 10.
Ten students are absent today and 15 students were absent yesterday. At most 10 students were absent in two consecutive days.

43. Solution: 640.
Method 1:
$(16+10)^2 - (16-10)^2 = (16+10+16-10)(16+10-16+10) = 32 \times 20 = 640$.

Method 2:
$(16+10)^2 - (16-10)^2 = 26^2 - 6^2 = (26-6)(26+6) = 20 \times 32 = 640$.

44. Solution: 84.
$\dfrac{24 \times 90 + 36 \times 80}{24 + 36} = 84$.

45. Solution: 800%.
$\dfrac{A_2}{A_1} = \dfrac{\pi r_2^2}{\pi r_1^2} = (\dfrac{r_2}{r_1})^2 = (\dfrac{3r_1}{r_1})^2 = 9 \quad \Rightarrow \quad A_2 = 9A_1 = A_1 + 8A_1 \Rightarrow \dfrac{A_2 - A_1}{A_1} = 8 = 800\%$

46. Solution: 1024.
$(17 - \sqrt{17^2 - 8^2})^{10} = (17 - \sqrt{15^2})^{10} = (17-15)^{10} = 2^{10} = 1024$.

47. Solution: 168.
$21 = 3 \times 7$
$14 = 2^2 \times 7$
$56 = 2^3 \times 7$
LCM (14, 21, 28) = $2^3 \times 7 \times 3 = 168$.

48. Solution: Tuesday.
Method 1:
We know that April 3 is a Friday. So April 4 is a Saturday. So does December 12. Thus December 15 is three days from Saturday, which is a Tuesday.

Method 2:
We know that April 3 is a Friday. So April 10 is also a Friday.
We count the number of days in the time periods:
April 10 – May 10 – June 10 – July 10 – August 10 – Sept 10 – Oct 10 – Nov 10 – Dec 10.
We get $30 + 31 + 30 + 31 + 31 + 30 + 31 + 30 = 244 = 34 \times 7 + 6$.
So December 10 is a Thursday. December 15 is Tuesday.

49. Solution: 23.
$437 = 1 \times 437 = 19 \times 23$.
We know that each case holds less than 20 discs. He needs to buy 23 cases.

50. Solution: 60 inches.
$\dfrac{5}{3+4+5} \times 144 = 60$

51. Solution: 6.
$4 - 1 = 3; \quad 4 - 2 = 2; \quad 4 - 3 = 1$
$1 - 4 = -3; \quad 1 - 3 = -2; \quad 1 - 2 = -1$.

52. Solution: 9:59.

53. Solution: 4.
By the midpoint formula,
$x = \dfrac{5-7}{2} = -1$, and $y = \dfrac{12-2}{2} = 5$.
$x + y = 4$.

54. Solution: Two revolutions.
The distance D traveled by the centre of the circle A can be used as a representative distance traveled by the circle A.
$D = 2\pi(r + r) = 4\pi r$.
The number of revolutions is $\dfrac{4\pi r}{2\pi r} = 2$.

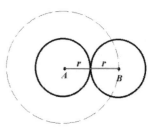

55. Solution: 328.
$2 + 3 + 5 + 7 + 11 + 13 + 17 + 19 + 23 + 29 + 31 + 37 + 41 + 43 + 47 +$

Mathcounts Speed and Accuracy Practice Tests Test 8

$= (47 + 3) + (43 + 7) + (37 + 13) + (31 + 19) + (29 + 11) + (23 + 17) + 41 + 2 + 5 = 50 \times 4 + 40 \times 2 + 48 = 328$.

56. Solution: 30.
Let the number be x.
$18 = \frac{60}{100} \times x \quad \Rightarrow \quad x = 30$.

57. Solution: 1.
Let d, n, and p be the number of dimes, nickels, and pennies, respectively.
$10d + 5n + p = 88$ \hfill (1)
$d + n + p = 7$ \hfill (2)
(1) − (2): $9d + 4n = 81 \quad \Rightarrow \quad d = 1 \bmod 4$.
d can be 1, 5, 9,...
Since the total number of coins is 7. d can only be 1.

58. Solution: 180.
Method 1:
We see that 9, 40 and 41 are the Pythagorean triples. The area is $9 \times 40 / 2 = 180$.

Method 2:
By Heron's formula, the area is
$\sqrt{p(p-a)(p-b)(p-c)} = \sqrt{45(45-9)(45-40)(45-41)} = \sqrt{45 \cdot 36 \cdot 5 \cdot 4} = 180$.

59. Solution: 3.
When A(−8, 5) is reflected across the x-axis, x coordinate keeps unchanged and y coordinate change the sign. So we have B(−8, −5).

When B(−8, −5) is reflected across the y-axis, y coordinate keeps unchanged and x coordinate change the sign. So we have C(8, −5). The sum is 8 − 5 = 3.

60. Solution: 1.
$\frac{5x^2 - 4y^2}{61} = \frac{5 \times 5^2 - 4 \times 4^2}{61} = \frac{5^3 - 4^3}{61} = \frac{(5-1)(5^2 + 5 \times 4 + 4^2)}{61} = \frac{61}{61} = 1$.

61. Solution: 32.
$512 \times 256 \times 128 \times 64 \times \frac{1}{2} \times \frac{1}{4} \times \frac{1}{8} \times \frac{1}{16} \times \frac{1}{32} \times \frac{1}{1024}$

$$= (512 \times \frac{1}{32})(256 \times \frac{1}{16})(128 \times \frac{1}{8})(64 \times \frac{1}{4}) \times \frac{1}{2} \times \frac{1}{1024}.$$
$$= 2^4 \times 2^4 \times 2^4 \times 2^4 \div 2^{11} = 2^{16-11} = 2^5 = 32$$

62. Solution: 20.
$n(A \text{ or } B) = n(A) + n(B) - n(A \text{ and } B) = 26 + 47 - 53 = 20.$

63. Solution: 85 minutes.
$\frac{48}{60} = \frac{68}{x} \quad \Rightarrow \quad x = 85 \text{ minutes.}$

64. Solution: −5/6.
$$\frac{\sqrt{3} \times \sqrt[3]{3^5}}{3^3} = (3)^{\frac{1}{2}} \times (3)^{\frac{5}{3}} \times (3)^{-3} = (3)^{\frac{1}{2} + \frac{5}{3} - 3} = 3^{-\frac{5}{6}}.$$
Thus $n = -5/6$.

65. Solution: 1/3600.
$\frac{10}{10 \times 3600} = \frac{1}{3600}.$

66. Solution: 56%.
$\frac{1.95 - 1.25}{1.25} = 0.56$

67. Solution: 234.
Let the total number of votes be x.
$x = 0.45 x + 0.4 x + 78 \quad \Rightarrow \quad x = 520.$ The answer is $520 \times 0.45 = 234.$

68. Solution: 400.
$(4 + 14 + 24 + 34) + (96 + 86 + 76 + 66) = (4 + 96) + (14 + 86) + (24 + 76) + (34 + 66) = 4 \times 100 = 400.$

69. Solution: 46.
Let x and y be the least and greatest of these integers.
$\frac{x + y}{2} = 23 \quad \Rightarrow \quad x + y = 46.$

70. Solution: 1600 %.

Let x side of the original triangle and y be the side of the new triangle.
Let A_2 area of the original triangle and A_1 be the area of the new triangle.
$$\frac{A_1}{A_2} = \left(\frac{x}{y}\right)^2 = \left(\frac{4x}{x}\right)^2 = 16$$
So the answer is 1600%.

71. Solution: 13.
$x = \frac{32.5}{100} \times 40 = 13$.

72. Solution: 2862.
1- digit numbers: $1 \times 9 = 9$
2- digit numbers: $2 \times 90 = 180$
3- digit numbers: $3 \times 891 = 2673$
The answer is $9 + 180 + 2673 = 2862$.

73. Solution: 5 pairs.
(43, 5), (41, 7), (37, 11), (31, 17), and (29, 19).

74. Solution: 3600.
Method 1:
$S = \frac{(1+120) \times 120}{2} = 7260$
$S_{even} = \frac{2(1+60) \times 60}{2} = 60 \times 61 = 3660$
$S_{odd} = S - S_{even} = 7260 - 3660 = 3600$.

Method 2:
$1 + 3 + 5 + 7 + \ldots + 2n - 1 = n^2$.
The answer is $1 + 3 + 5 + 7 + \ldots = 60^2 = 3600$.

75. Solution: 3.
Let the number be x.
$x \geq x^2 - 6 \quad \Rightarrow \quad x^2 - x - 6 \leq 0 \quad \Rightarrow$
$(x+2)(x-3) \leq 0$.

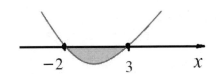

The greatest real number is 3.

Mathcounts Speed and Accuracy Practice Tests   Test 8

76. Solution: Saturday.

Tuesday	Wednesday	Thursday	Friday	Saturday	...
7					
14					
21	22	23	24	25	

So the 25th day is a Saturday.

77. Solution: 12:00.

$$\begin{array}{r} 9:45 \\ +\ 2:15 \\ \hline 12:00 \end{array}$$

Note that 40 + 10 + 10 = 60 minutes = 1 hour.

78. Solution: 2015.

$2^{2016} - 2^{2015} = 2^x \quad \Rightarrow \quad 2^{2015}(2-1) = 2^x \quad \Rightarrow \quad 2^{2015} = 2^x$.

So $x = 2015$.

79. Solution: 63/64.

Let $S = \dfrac{1}{2} + \dfrac{1}{4} + \dfrac{1}{8} + \dfrac{1}{16} + \dfrac{1}{32} + \dfrac{1}{64}$ \hfill (1)

(1) × 64: $64S = (\dfrac{1}{2} + \dfrac{1}{4} + \dfrac{1}{8} + \dfrac{1}{16} + \dfrac{1}{32} + \dfrac{1}{64}) \times 64 = 32 + 16 + 8 + 4 + 2 + 1 = 63$.

So $S = 63/64$.

80. Solution: 44.

The minute hand moves 360 degrees in 60 minutes, or 6 degrees per minute. The hour hand moves 360 degrees in 12 hours or 0.5 degrees per minute. Since the minute hand travels 5.5 degrees per minute faster than the hour hand, it gains 90 degrees every 90/5.5 minutes. In 24 hours (1440 minutes) 90 degrees is gained 1440/(90/5.5) = 88 times. For half of these times, the angular difference between the hands is 180 or zero degrees. The hands are at a right angle the remaining 44 times.

MATHCOUNTS

■ Speed and Accuracy Practice Test 9 ■

Name

Date

DO NOT BEGIN UNTIL YOU ARE INSTRUCTED TO DO SO.
The test consists of two parts, with each part 40 problems. You will have 15 minutes to complete the part 1 and 25 minutes to complete the part 2. You are not allowed to use calculators, books, or any other aids during this round. Calculations may be done on scratch paper. All answers must be complete, legible, and simplified to lowest terms. Record only final answers. Do each problem as quick as you can. If you finish one problem, go to the next. Do not spend any time to check your answers.

	Total Correct	Scorer's Initials
Part I		
Part II		

©www.mymathcounts.com

Mathcounts Speed and Accuracy Practice Test 9

Part I Problems 1–40

Mathcounts Speed and Accuracy Practice Tests — Test 9

1. $192 + 59 + 18 =$

2. $17^2 =$

3. $101 \times 21 =$

4. $20.46 - 3.76 =$

5. $20 - 4^3 \div 8 =$

6. $\frac{1}{2}$ of $(\frac{1}{2} + 1\frac{1}{2}) =$

7. Write 6.1% as a decimal.

8. Write $\frac{1}{5} \times \frac{6}{7} \times \frac{7}{8}$ as a percent.

9. If $.0000043 = 4.3 \times 10^n$, then $n =$

10. $\sqrt{(-1-3)^2 + (-2-1)^2} =$

11. 19 weeks = —— days

12. The mean of 133, 134, 135, 136, 137, 138, 139 =

13. $4\frac{5}{17} \times 17 =$

14. $7! =$

15. If 5 cookies cost $4.45, then one cookie costs —— ¢

16. If $\frac{4}{5} = \frac{2x}{5}$, then $x =$

17. If $a = 40$, $b = -5$ and $c = 2$, then $\frac{a}{b} \div c =$

18. Express 60 miles per hour as ft per second.

19. Express $\dfrac{\pi \cdot 7^2 - \pi \cdot 1^2}{\pi \cdot 10^2}$ as a simplest fraction.

20. Write $9\frac{1}{5} \times 9\frac{4}{5}$ as a mixed umber.

21. The complement of an 79° angle is ——°

22. Simply $\dfrac{\frac{5}{2} - 4}{\frac{5}{2}}$.

Mathcounts Speed and Accuracy Practice Tests   Test 9

23. The largest palindrome smaller than 1438 is

24. If $x = 2$ and $y = 5$, find the value of $3x - y$.

25. $3 + 6 + 9 + 12 + 15 + 18 + 21 =$

26. $7^2 + 24^2 =$

27. If $x^2 = 15$ and $x < 0$, then $x =$

28. $12\text{ft} \times 5\text{ft} \times 9\text{ft} = \underline{} \text{yds}^3$

29. The 3rd triangular number is

30. If $f(x) = (x - 17)^3$, the $f(12) =$

31. Calculate
$\pi(2\sqrt{2})^2 - \dfrac{1}{2} \cdot 2\sqrt{2} \cdot 2\sqrt{2} - \dfrac{1}{2} \cdot 2 \cdot 2 =$

32. Compute: $\dfrac{20 + 4 + 12}{\dfrac{45}{60} + \dfrac{47}{60} + \dfrac{58}{60}}$. Express the answer as a simplified fraction.

33. If $(2x + 7)(x - 10) = 2x^2 + ax - 70$, then $a =$

34. Find x if $17 + x + 2x + 4x + 5x = 53$.

35. The volume of a cube with edge $\sqrt{2}$ is

36. Simplify $\dfrac{72}{380} + \dfrac{2}{380}$

37. The difference between the supplement and the complement of a 49° angle is —°

38. $6^4 =$

39. The slope of the line passing through (0,7) and (7,1) is

40. $86_9 - 58_9 =$ ——

Mathcounts Speed and Accuracy Practice Test 9

Part II Problems 41–80

41. Solve for n: $(2^{2n} \cdot 5^2)^2 = 10{,}000$

42. Find the sum of the following numbers. Express your answer to the nearest thousandth: $\sqrt{2}$, π, e, 1.414, 3.142, 2.718.

43. How many solutions does the equation $\sqrt{5x} = x\sqrt{5}$ have?

44. If $n \times 6! = 7!$, then what is value of n?

45. If $a \star b = a^b + b^a$, for all positive integer values of a and b, then what is the value of $5 \star 4$?

46. Each bounce of a ball goes 1/3 as high as the previous bounce. The second bounce was 24 inches high. What was the height, in inches, of the first bounce?

47. The perimeter of an isosceles triangle is 16 cm, and the altitude to its base is 4 cm. What is the number of square centimeters in the area of the triangle?

48. There are 50 equally-weighted questions on Mr. Smith's math final. If a student must score 93% or greater to get an "A", what is the minimum number of questions that must be answered correctly to pass?

49. A pizza parlor offers six toppings. What is the greatest number of three-topping pizzas that can be made such that no two pizzas have the same topping combination?

50. Jack bought a CD for $11 and sold it for $21. He then bought it back for $29 and sold it again for $28. How many dollars profit did he make?

51. What is 150% of 0.86, to the nearest hundredth?

52. Given $\dfrac{x}{y} = \dfrac{3}{5}$ and $\dfrac{y}{z} = \dfrac{5}{3}$, what is the value of x/z?

53. What is the greatest odd integer that is a factor of $6!$?

54. What is the number of centimeters in the diameter of a circle whose area is $100\pi^3$ cm^2?

55. Compute: $2015 \div 2015\dfrac{2015}{2016}$. Express your answer as a common fraction.

56. One leg of a right triangle is increased by 20%, and the other leg is decreased by 20%. By what percent does the area of the triangle decrease?

57. Data can be entered at the rate of 150 pieces of information in 12 minutes. At this rate, how many pieces of information can be entered in 2 1/2 hours?

58. A portion of a number line is divided into 3, as shown. $AB = 8$, $AP = 5$, and $OB = 6$. Find OP.

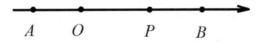

59. Ralph can do two-third of a job in one-thirds of an hour. At this rate, how many hours will it take him to finish the entire job?

60. Today is April 30th. What month will it be 100 months from now?

61. It is known that $\dfrac{9n}{n+1} > 8$ and n is a positive integer. What is the least possible value for n?

62. Twenty cards, numbered 1-20, are placed in a box. One card is randomly selected. What is the probability that the number on the card is prime and is a multiple of 5? Express your answer as a common fraction.

63. As shown in the figure, a, b, and c are real numbers. Simplify $|b-a|+|a-c|+|c-b|$.

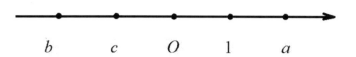

64. During his morning commute to work in rush traffic, Bob's average speed was 3 km per hour. During his afternoon commute back home along the same route, his average speed was 5 km per hour. The distance from his house to his office is 10 km. What was his average speed for the entire round trip? Express your answer as a common fraction.

65. A rectangle has perimeter 50 inches and integer length sides, in inches. What is the number of square inches in the greatest possible area?

66. What is 1/2 of 1/3 of 1/5 of 300?

67. What is the value of x in the equation $\dfrac{\frac{2}{3}+\frac{1}{5}}{13}=\dfrac{1}{x}$?

68. Six boys and three girls are seating nine chairs in a row. The girls arrive before the boys and decide to choose their chairs so that each girl will be between two boys. In how many ways can girls choose their chairs?

69. What is the greatest common factor of 102 and 114?

70. The angle measures of the three angles of a triangle are in the ratio 1:3:6. What is the number of degrees in the measure of the smallest angle?

Mathcounts Speed and Accuracy Practice Tests   Test 9

71. What is the least common multiple of 1, 2, 3, 4, 5, 6, 7, 8, and 9?

72. Express as a common fraction: $\sqrt{7\frac{1}{9}}$.

73. The number 119 can be written as $13q + r$ where q and r are integers and $0 < r < 13$. What is the value of $q - r$?

74. How many seconds are in $2\frac{1}{9}$ hours?

75. If Mike drinks four 16-ounce glasses of water each day during 2015, how many gallons of water will he consume? (A gallon is 128 ounces.) Express your answer as a decimal to the nearest tenth.

76. Two opposite sides of a square are each increased by 50%, while the other two sides are each decreased by 30%. The area of the original square is increased by what percent?

77. A rectangle has an area of 60 m² and the perimeter of 34 m. What is the number of meters in the diagonal of the rectangle?

78. As shown in the figure, the solid is formed by gluing six unit cubes together. What is the number of square units of the surface area of the solid?

79. What is the greatest possible value of $x - y$ if $x^2 - y^2 = 1991$? Both x and y are positive integers.

80. Box A contains 18 cards, numbered 1- 18. Box B contains 18 cards, numbered 19-36. Alex reaches in box A and draws out x cards at one time. Bob reaches in box B and draws out $3x - 6$ cards at one time. The number of ways Alex draws x cards from box A is the same as the number of ways Bob draws $3x - 6$ cards from box B. What is the sum of all possible values for x ?

Mathcounts Speed and Accuracy Practice Tests Test 9

Answer Keys:

Part I:

1. 269
2. 289
3. 2121
4. 16.7
5. 12
6. 1
7. 0.061
8. 15%
9. −6
10. $\sqrt{16+9} = 5$
11. 133
12. 136
13. 73
14. 5040
15. ¢89
16. 2
17. − 4
18. 88.
19. 12/25
20. $90\frac{4}{25}$
21. 11
22. $\frac{-3}{5}$
23. 1331
24. 1
25. 74
26. 625
27. $-\sqrt{15}$
28. 20
29. 6
30. − 125
31. $8\pi - 6$.
32. 72/5
33. −13
34. $x = 3$.
35. $2\sqrt{2}$
36. 37/190.
37. 90
38. 1296
39. $-\frac{6}{7}$
40. 27_9

Mathcounts Speed and Accuracy Practice Tests — Test 9

PART II

41. 1.

42. 14.548.

43. 2.

44. 7.

45. 1649.

46. 72.

47. 12.

48. 47.

49. 20.

50. $9.

51. 1.29.

52. 1.

53. 45.

54. 20π.

55. $\dfrac{2016}{2017}$.

56. 4 %.

57. 1875.

58. 3.

59. $\dfrac{1}{2}$ hours.

60. August.

61. 9.

62. 1/20.

63. $2(a-b)$.

64. $\dfrac{15}{4}$.

65. 156.

66. 10.

67. 15.

68. 60.

69. 6.

70. 18°.

71. 2520.

72. 8/3.

73. 7.

74. 7600 seconds.

75. 182.5.

76. 5%.

77. 13.

78. 34 square units.

79. 11.

80. 9.

Mathcounts Speed and Accuracy Practice Tests — Test 9

Solutions to Part II:

41. Solution: 1.
$(2^{2n} \cdot 5^2)^2 = 100{,}000 \Rightarrow 2^{4n} \cdot 5^4 = 2^4 \cdot 5^4 \Rightarrow 2^{4n} = 2^4 \Rightarrow 4n = 4 \Rightarrow n = 1$.

42. Solution: 14.548.
$\sqrt{2} + \pi + e + 1.414 + 3.142 + 2.718 = 2(1.414 + 3.142 + 2.718) = 14.548$.

43. Solution: 2.
Square both sides of equation $\sqrt{5x} = x\sqrt{5}$: $5x = 5x^2 \Rightarrow x^2 - x = 0 \Rightarrow x(x-1) = 0$. $x = 1$ or $x = 0$. So we have two solutions.

44. Solution: 7.
$n \times 6! = 7! \Rightarrow n \times 6! = 7 \times 6! \Rightarrow n = 7$

45. Solution: 1649.
$5 \star 4 = 5^4 + 4^5 = 625 + 1024 = 1649$.

46. Solution: 72.
Let the first bounce be x.
$(1/3)x = 24 \Rightarrow x = 72$.

47. Solution: 12.
As shown in the figure, we can write:
$2b + a = 16$ \hfill (1)
Applying Pythagorean Theorem to the right triangle ACD:
$b^2 - (\frac{a}{2})^2 = 4^2 \Rightarrow (2b)^2 - (a)^2 = 4 \times 4^2$
$\Rightarrow (2b+a)(2b-a) = 64$ \hfill (2)

Substituting (1) into (2): $2b - a = 4$ \hfill (3)
(1) − (2): $2a = 12$, which is exactly the area of the triangle.

48. Solution: 47.
By proportion: $\dfrac{50}{100} = \dfrac{x}{93} \Rightarrow x = \dfrac{50}{100} \times 93 = 46.5 \approx 47$.

49. Solution: 20.

We select 3 toppings from 6 toppings. Order does not matter.
$$\binom{6}{3} = \frac{6 \times 5 \times 4}{3 \times 2 \times 1} = 20$$

50. Solution: $9.
The total amount of money he paid is 11 + 29 = 40.
The total amount of money he received is 21 + 28 = 49.
The profit is 49 - 40 = $9.

51. Solution: 1.29.
$$\frac{15}{100} \times 0.86 = 1.29$$

52. Solution: 1.
Method 1:
$$\frac{x}{y} = \frac{3}{5} \qquad (1)$$

$$\frac{y}{z} = \frac{5}{3} \qquad (2)$$

(1) ÷ (2): $\frac{x}{z} = 1$.

Method 2:
$$\frac{x}{y} = \frac{3}{5} \qquad (1)$$

$$\frac{y}{z} = \frac{5}{3} \quad \Rightarrow \quad \frac{z}{y} = \frac{3}{5} \qquad (2)$$

Comparing (1) and (2) we see that $x = z$. So $\frac{x}{z} = 1$.

53. Solution: 45.
6! = 6 × 5 × 4 × 3 × 2 × 1. The greatest odd integer factor is 3 × 5 × 3 = 45.

54. Solution: 20π.
$$\frac{\pi}{4} d^2 = 100\pi^3 \quad \Rightarrow \quad d^2 = 400\pi^2 \quad \Rightarrow \quad d = 20\pi$$

55. Solution: $\frac{2016}{2017}$.

Mathcounts Speed and Accuracy Practice Tests Test 9

$$2015 \div 2015\frac{2015}{2016} = 2015 \div \frac{2015 \times 2016 + 2015}{2016} = 2015 \div \frac{2015 \times 2017}{2016}$$
$$= 2015 \times \frac{2016}{2015 \times 2017} = \frac{2016}{2017}$$

56. Solution: 4 %.
Let the legs be a and b.
$\frac{1.2a \times .08b}{2} = 0.96 \times \frac{ab}{2}$. The area of the triangle decreases by $1 - 0.96 = 0.04 = 4\%$.

57. Solution: 1875.
Let x be the pieces of information can be entered.
We sue the proportion: $\frac{150}{12} = \frac{x}{120 + 30}$ $\Rightarrow$ $x = 1875$

58. Solution: 3.
Method 1:
$OP = OB - PB = OB - (AB - AP) = 6 - (8 - 5) = 3$.

Method 2:
We know that $AB = 8$ and $AP = 5$. So $PB = 3$. Since $OB = 6$, $OP = 3$.

59. Solution: $\frac{1}{2}$ hours.

$\frac{\frac{2}{3}}{\frac{1}{3}} = \frac{1}{x}$ $\Rightarrow$ $x = \frac{\frac{1}{3}}{\frac{2}{3}} = \frac{1}{2}$.

60. Solution: August.
$100 = 12 \times 8 + 4$.
Four months from now will be August.

61. Solution: 9.
$\frac{9n}{n+1} > 8$ $\Rightarrow$ $9n > 8(n+1)$ $\Rightarrow$ $n > 8$.
The least possible value for n is 9.

Mathcounts Speed and Accuracy Practice Tests — Test 9

62. Solution: 1/20.
There is only one card satisfying the requirement: 5. So the probability is 1/20.

63. Solution: $2(a-b)$.
$|b-a|+|a-c|+|c-b| = |a-b|+|a-c|+|c-b| = a-b+a-c+c-b = 2(a-b)$

64. Solution: $\dfrac{15}{4}$.
Let v be the average speed for the entire round trip.
$v = \dfrac{2 \times 10}{\dfrac{10}{3}+\dfrac{10}{5}} = \dfrac{15}{4}$.

65. Solution: 156.
Let a and b be the length and width of the rectangle, respectively.
$2(a+b) = 50 \quad \Rightarrow \quad a+b = 25$.
The greatest area is obtained when a and b are as close as possible. So $a = 12$ and $b = 13$. The greatest area is $12 \times 13 = 156$.

66. Solution: 10.
$\dfrac{1}{2} \times \dfrac{1}{3} \times \dfrac{1}{5} \times 300 = 10$.

67. Solution: 15.
$\dfrac{\dfrac{2}{3}+\dfrac{1}{5}}{13} = \dfrac{\dfrac{13}{15}}{13} = \dfrac{1}{15}$. So $x = 15$,

68. Solution: 60.
We sit the boys first. Once the boys are seated, there are five spaces for three girls to choose $\binom{5}{3}$ (the two spaces at the ends do not count because each girl needs to sit between two boys) and there are 3! ways for them to rearrange themselves.

Mathcounts Speed and Accuracy Practice Tests   Test 9

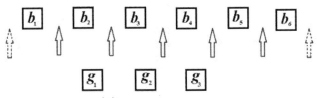

By the product rule, the answer is $\binom{5}{3} \times 3! = 60$.

69. Solution: 6.
$102 = 2 \times 51 = 2 \times 3 \times 17$
$114 = 2 \times 57 = 2 \times 3 \times 19$
The answer is $2 \times 3 = 6$.

70. Solution: 18°.
Method 1:
By proportion:
$\frac{1}{1+3+6} \times 180 = 18°$.

Method 2:
By solving the equation: $x + 3x + 6x = 180° \Rightarrow x = 18°$.

71. Solution: 2520.
lcm $= 2^3 \times 3^2 \times 5 \times 7 = 2520$.

72. Solution: 8/3.
$\sqrt{7\frac{1}{9}} = \sqrt{\frac{64}{9}} = \frac{8}{3}$.

73. Solution: 7.
$119 = 13 \times 9 + 2$.
$q - r = 9 - 2 = 7$.

74. Solution: 7600 seconds.
1 hour = 3600 seconds.
$2\frac{1}{9} \times 3600 = \frac{19}{9} \times 3600 = 19 \times 400 = 7600$ seconds.

75. Solution: 182.5.
$$\frac{4 \times 16 \times 365}{128} = 182.5.$$

76. Solution: 5%.
Let the side be a.
$1.5\,a \times 0.7a = 1.05\,a^2$. So the area of the original square is increased by 5 percent.

77. Solution: 13.
Let the sides of the rectangle be a and b.
$2(a + b) = 34 \Rightarrow a + b = 17 \Rightarrow (a+b) = 17^2$ (1)
$ab = 60 \Rightarrow 2ab = 120$ (2)
(1) − (2): $a^2 + b^2 = 169 = 13^2 = c^2$.
The diagonal is 13 m.

78. Solution: 34 square units.
We view this solid from three directions: front view, side view, and top view. We get $2 \times 5 + 2 \times 5 + 2 \times 6 = 32$.

79. Solution: 11.
$x^2 - y^2 = 1991 \Rightarrow x^2 - y^2 = (x-y)(x+y) = 181 \times 11$.
Since 181 is a prime number and $x + y > x - y$, the greatest possible value of $x - y$ is 11.

80. Solution: 9.
The number of ways Alex draws x cards from box A is $\binom{18}{x}$

The number of ways Bob draws $3x - 6$ cards from box A is $\binom{18}{3x-6}$.

So we set up the equation: $\binom{18}{x} = \binom{18}{3x-6}$ (1)

We have $x = 3x - 6$ (2)
or $x + 3x - 6 = 18$ (3)
with $0 \le x \le 18$ and $0 \le 3x - 6 \le 18$
Solving (2) and (3) we get: $x = 3$ and $x = 6$. Both are solutions of (1).
So the answer is $3 + 6 = 9$.

MATHCOUNTS

■ **Speed and Accuracy Practice Test 10**■

Name _____

Date _____

DO NOT BEGIN UNTIL YOU ARE INSTRUCTED TO DO SO.
The test consists of two parts, with each part 40 problems. You will have 15 minutes to complete the part 1 and 25 minutes to complete the part 2. You are not allowed to use calculators, books, or any other aids during this round. Calculations may be done on scratch paper. All answers must be complete, legible, and simplified to lowest terms. Record only final answers. Do each problem as quick as you can. If you finish one problem, go to the next. Do not spend any time to check your answers.

	Total Correct	Scorer's Initials
Part I		
Part II		

©www.mymathcounts.com

Mathcounts Speed and Accuracy Practice Test 10

Part I Problems 1–40

Mathcounts Speed and Accuracy Practice Tests — Test 10

1. $48 + 173 + 269 =$

2. $59.8 \times 11 =$

3. $64.8 - 33.8 =$

4. $17^2 =$

5. $127 \times 50 =$

6. $101 \times 68 =$

7. Find the remainder for $5372 \div 9$.

8. $25_6 + 42_6 =$

9. $32 \div 8 + 11 \times 6 =$

10. $\sqrt{324} =$

11. Express 3 miles in feet.

12. $19 \times 37 - 37 \times 15 =$

13. If $\frac{1}{2}x + 8 = 35$, then $x = ?$

14. 23 feet = ——— yards. Express your answer as a mixed number.

15. The area of a triangle with base 22 and height 2.5 is ———. Express your answer as a common fraction.

16. The mean of 73, 77, 78 and 76 is ———

17. $125 \times 16 =$

18. $111 \times 151 =$

19. $98 \times 96 =$

20. $4\frac{1}{3} \times 27 =$

21. Express $8\frac{3}{4} \times 8\frac{1}{4}$ as a mixed number.

22. One sq. mile = ——— acres

23. $37^2 \div 5$ has a remainder of ———

24. Find an interior angle of a regular undecagon (hendecagon) in degree.

25. Express $\frac{5}{8} + \frac{8}{5}$ as a mixed number

26. If $x^2 = 15$ and $x > 0$, then $x =$

27. Find the area of a square with diagonal 5. Express your answer as a mixed number.

Mathcounts Speed and Accuracy Practice Tests — Test 10

28. Express 35_7 in base 10.

29. Find the area of a circle with radius 10.

30. Find the number of diagonals that can be drawn from one vertex of a octagon.

31. Find the sum of the three angles of a scalene obtuse triangle in degree.

32. Simplify $\sqrt{48}$.

33. Find b if $43_b = 31_{10}$.

34. Find the volume of a cube with edge 7.

35. What is the slope of the line passing (4,8) and (−2,4)?

36. What is the speed of 60 mi/hr in ft/sec?

37. What number is halfway between 7 and −13?

38. Find the value of $7! \div 5!$.

39. What is the measure of an exterior angle of a regular pentagon in degree?

40. Express as a common fraction in simplest form: $0.\overline{11} + 0.\overline{22}$.

Mathcounts Speed and Accuracy Practice Test 10

Part II Problems 41–80

Mathcounts Speed and Accuracy Practice Tests — Test 10

41. Sami began a math contest at 10:37 a.m. and finished at 1:19 p.m. the same day. How many minutes did she take to complete the contest?

42. If $3x + 8 = 23$, what is the value of $3x + 3$?

43. Three out of every five students at Gauss Middle School went to the Spring Fling. If 100 students did not go to the Spring Fling, how many students attend this school?

44. Each edge length of a cube is doubled. How many times the volume of the new cube is the volume of the original cube?

45. What is the sum of the first four prime numbers greater than 100?

46. If x is an integer such that $12 > x > 3$, what is the greatest value of $11x + 11$?

47. Two congruent isosceles right triangles are joined to create this figure. Each leg of each triangle measures 5 units. What is the total area of the figure, in square units?

48. If the sum of the digits of a positive two-digit integer is 17, what is the probability that none of the digits is 9?

49. A right triangle has a hypotenuse of 26 units. If one leg is 10, what is the sum of the lengths of the legs, in units?

50. The length of a right, rectangular prism is tripled, its width is quadrupled and its height is doubled. What is the ratio of the original volume to the new volume? Express your answer as a common fraction.

Mathcounts Speed and Accuracy Practice Tests   Test 10

51. If $n + (1/n) = 5$, what is the value of $n^2 - 5n$?

52. The endpoints of segment BC are $B(-5, 4)$ and $C(5, 6)$. What is the product of the coordinates of the midpoint of segment BC?

53. Given $a + b = 16$, $b + c = 19$ and $a + c = 13$, what is the sum of a, b and c?

54. What is the sum of the distinct prime divisors of $17 + 17^2$?

55. If $3^n = 27^3$, what is the integer value of n?

56. If a 12-hour analog clock reads 10:00, what is the degree measure of the larger angle formed by the minute and hour hands?

57. The probability that Alex will draw a yellow marble at random from a bag containing yellow marbles and blue marbles is 3/5. If 21 of the marbles are yellow, how many marbles are blue?

58. What is the area, in square units, of an equilateral triangle whose side is $2\sqrt[4]{3}$?

59. What is the value of the digit K that will make the number $5K6$ divisible by 9?

60. James can paint a wall in 10 minutes, and Evan can paint the same size wall in 20 minutes. If they work together, how many minutes will it take them to paint fifteen walls of this size?

61. Joe and Mike live 30 miles from each other at opposite ends of Highway 11. They drive toward each other on Highway 11 at the same time. Joe travels at an average speed of 40 mph and Mike travels at an average speed of 60 mph. How many minutes will it take for them to meet?

Mathcounts Speed and Accuracy Practice Tests — Test 10

62. The *GCF* of two numbers is 7. Their product is 1,001. What is the *LCM* of the two numbers?

63. Eight distinct points are arranged on a circle. How many different triangles are there whose three vertices are among those eight points?

64. A store advertised a computer at 50% off plus an additional 50% off the sale price. Erich paid $75 before taxes, what was the original price of the computer?

65. Meili bought a box of dog biscuits for her golden retriever Kara. She gives Kara 7 dog biscuits a day. After seventeen days she counted 91 biscuits left in the box. What is the number of dog biscuits in the box originally?

66. How many different games need to be played so that 5 teams each play each other exactly twice?

67. Find the total surface area of a 3 by 3 by 3 cube.

68. The graph of the line $\frac{x}{a} + \frac{y}{b} = 1$ is shown. What is the value of $b - a$?

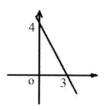

69. If $4x + y = 17$ and $x + 4y = 8$, what is the value of $5x + 5y$?

70. What is the arithmetic mean of the first five prime numbers? Express your answer as a mixed number.

Mathcounts Speed and Accuracy Practice Tests — Test 10

71. The number line shown has uniformly-spaced markings. If point P is equidistant from its two closest markings, what is the coordinate of P? Express your answer as a common fraction.

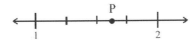

72. What is the smallest positive integer that can be added to the sum of the consecutive integers $(1 + 2 + \ldots + 10 + 11)$ so that the resulting total is divisible by 7?

73. When 50 is increased by 50% it then is equal to what number decreased by 25%?

74. Two fair, standard six-sided dice are rolled. What is the probability that the sum of two numbers is a prime number greater than 5? Express your answer as a common fraction.

75. Given a right triangle whose side lengths are all integer multiples of 11, how many units are in the smallest possible perimeter of such a triangle?

76. The average age of six students in a room is 15 years. A 10-year-old student leaves the room. What is the average age of the five remaining students, in years?

77. If the ratio of $5x$ to $2y$ is $5/6$, what is the ratio of $2x$ to $5y$? Express your answer as a common fraction.

78. How many integers x, such that $1 \leq x \leq 1000$, are multiples of 13?

79. What is the greatest common factor of 221 and 247?

80. What is the product of $\sqrt[3]{49}$ and $\sqrt[6]{49}$?

Mathcounts Speed and Accuracy Practice Tests — Test 10

Answer Keys

Part I

1. 490
2. 657.8
3. 31
4. 289
5. 6350
6. 6868
7. 8
8. 111
9. 70
10. 18
11. 15840 ft.
12. 148
13. 54
14. $7\frac{2}{3}$
15. $\frac{55}{2}$.
16. 76
17. 2000
18. 16,761
19. 9408
20. 117
21. $72\frac{3}{16}$
22. 640
23. 4
24. 147°.
25. $2\frac{9}{40}$
26. $x = \sqrt{15}$
27. $12\frac{1}{2}$.
28. 26_{10}.
29. 100π
30. 5
31. 180°.
32. $4\sqrt{3}$
33. 7.
34. 343.
35. $\frac{2}{3}$
36. 88
37. -3
38. 42
39. 72°
40. 1/3.

Mathcounts Speed and Accuracy Practice Tests   **Test 10**

Part II:

41. 162 (minutes)
42. 18.
43. 250 (students)
44. 8 (times)
45. 420.
46. 132
47. 25 (sq units)
48. 0.
49. 34 (units)
50. 1/24
51. −1.
52. 0.
53. 24.
54. 22
55. 9.
56. 300 (degrees)
57. 14 (blue marbles).
58. 3 (sq units)
59. 7.
60. 100 (minutes)
61. 18 minutes.
62. 143.
63. 56 (triangles)
64. 300 (dollars)
65. 210.
66. 20 (games)
67. 54.
68. 1
69. 25.
70. $5\frac{3}{5}$.
71. 13/8.
72. 4
73. 100
74. 2/9.
75. 132 (units)
76. 16 (years)
77. 2/15.
78. 76 (integers)
79. 13.
80. 7.

Mathcounts Speed and Accuracy Practice Tests Test 10

Solutions to Part II:

41. Solution: 162 (minutes).
Method 1:
It takes 120 minutes from 10:37 a.m. to 12:37 p.m. There are $79 - 37 = 42$ minutes from 12:37 to 1:19. The answer is then $120 + 42 = 162$ minutes.

Method 2:
It takes 180 minutes from 10:37 a.m. to 1:37 p.m. There are $37 - 19 = 18$ minutes. The answer is then $1890 - 18 = 162$ minutes.

42. Solution: 18.
$3x + 3 = 3x + 8 - 5 = 23 - 5 = 18$.

43. Solution: 250.
We know that three out of every five students at Gauss Middle School went to the Spring Fling. So two out of every five students did not go. Let x be the total number of students.
$$\frac{2}{5} = \frac{100}{x} \implies x = 250.$$

44. Solution: 8.
Let V_1 be the original volume and V_2 be the new volume.
$$\frac{V_1}{V_2} = (\frac{a_1}{a_2})^3 = (\frac{1}{2})^3 = \frac{1}{8} \qquad V_2 = 8\, V_2.$$

45. Solution: 420.
$101 + 103 + 107 + 109 = 420$.

46. Solution: 132.
The greatest value of x is 11. $11x + 11 = 11 \times 11 + 11 = 11 \times 12 = 132$.

47. Solution: 25.
The total area of the figure, in square units, is $\frac{5 \times 5}{2} \times 2 = 25$.

48. Solution: 0.
$17 = 9 + 8$. So one digit must be 9. The probability that none of the digits is 9 will be 0.

49. 34.

Method 1:
By Pythagorean Theorem, $a^2 + b^2 = c^2 \Rightarrow a^2 + 10^2 = 26^2 \Rightarrow a = \sqrt{26^2 - 10^2} = 24$.
The sum of the legs is $10 + 24 = 34$.

Method 2:
This is a $5n$–$12n$–$13n$ right triangle. $n = 2$. So the answer is $10 + 24 = 34$.

50. Solution: $\dfrac{1}{24}$.

$\dfrac{V_1}{V_2} = \dfrac{l \times w \times h}{3l \times 4w \times 2h} = \dfrac{1}{24}$.

51. Solution: -1.
Multiplying n by both sides of $n + (1/n) = 5$: $n^2 + 1 = 5n \Rightarrow n^2 - 5n = -1$.

52. Solution: 0.
By the middle point formula, $x = \dfrac{x_1 + x_2}{2} = \dfrac{-5 + 5}{2} = 0$.
We know that product is zero without calculating y coordinate.

53. Solution: 24.
$a + b = 16$ (1)
$b + c = 19$ (2)
$a + c = 13$ (3)
(1) + (2) + (3): $2(a + b + c) = 48 \Rightarrow a + b + c = 24$.

54. Solution: 22.
$17 + 17^2 = 17(1 + 17) = 17 \times 18 = 17 \times 2 \times 3 \times 3$.
The sum of the distinct prime divisors is $17 + 2 + 3 = 22$.

55. Solution: 9.
$3^n = 27^3$ can be written as $3^n = 3^9$. Thus $n = 9$.

56. Solution: 300°.
The smaller angle is 60° and the larger angle is 360° − 60° = 300°

57. Solution: 14.

$$P = \frac{3}{5} = \frac{\binom{21}{1}}{\binom{21+b}{1}} \quad \Rightarrow \quad \frac{3}{5} = \frac{21}{21+b} \quad b = 14$$

58. Solution: 3.

The area of an equilateral triangle is: $A = \frac{\sqrt{3}}{4}a^2$. We know that $a = 2\sqrt[4]{3}$.

$A = \frac{\sqrt{3}}{4}(2\sqrt[4]{3})^2 = 3$.

59. Solution: 7.
The sum of the digits must be divisible by 9.
$5 + K + 6$ must be divisible by 9, or $2 + K$ must be divisible by 9. So $K = 7$.

60. Solution: 100 minutes.
James' rate is 1/10 and Evan's rate is 1/20.
Let t be the time they can finish the 15 walls when they work together, we have
$(\frac{1}{10} + \frac{1}{20}) \times t = 15 \quad \Rightarrow \quad t = 100$ minutes.

61. Solution: 18 minutes.
Let t be the time it takes for them to meet.
$(\frac{40}{60} + \frac{60}{60}) \times t = 30 \quad \Rightarrow \quad t = 18$ minutes.

62. Solution: 143.
Let two numbers be a and b.
$GCF(a, b) \times LCM(a, b) = a \times b \Rightarrow 7 \times LCM(a, b) = 1001 \Rightarrow LCM(a, b) = 143$.

63. Solution: 56.
We can form a triangle by connecting three points.
$\binom{8}{3} = \frac{8 \times 7 \times 6}{3 \times 2 \times 1} = 56$.

64. Solution: $300.

Let the original price be x.
$50\% \times 50\% \times x = 75$ $\Rightarrow$ $x = 300$.

65. Solution: 210.
$7 \times 17 + 91 = 210$

66. Solution: 20.
$2 \times \binom{5}{2} = 20$.

67. Solution: 54.
$6(3 \times 3) = 54$.

68. Solution: 1.
$b = 4, a = 3$.
$b - a = 1$.

69. Solution: 25.
$4x + y = 17$ (1)
$x + 4y = 8$ (2)
(1) + (2): $5x + 5y = 25$.

70. Solution: $5\frac{3}{5}$.
$(2 + 3 + 5 + 7 + 11)/5 = 28/5 = 5\frac{3}{5}$.

71. Solution: 13/8.
$x_P = \dfrac{x_A + x_B}{2} = \dfrac{1.5 + 1.75}{2} = 1.625 = 13/8$.

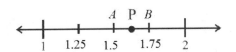

72. Solution: 4.
$1 + 2 + \ldots + 10 + 11 = \dfrac{(1+11) \times 11}{2} = 66$.

$66 + 4 = 70$ which is divisible by 7. So the answer is 4.

73. Solution: 100.
$50 \times 1.5 = x \times 0.75$ $\Rightarrow$ $x = 100$.

74. Solution: 2/9.

Mathcounts Speed and Accuracy Practice Tests **Test 10**

The sum of two numbers at most can be 12.
Prime numbers greater than 5 are 7 and 11.
7 = 6 + 1 = 1 + 6 = 5 + 2 = 2 + 5 = 4 + 3 = 3 + 4.
11 = 6 + 5 = 5 + 6.
The probability is 8/36 = 2/9.

75. Solution: 132.
Let the three sides be $11a$, $11b$, and $11c$, with $11c$ the longest side. The perimeter is $(11a + 11b + 11c) = 11(a + b + c) = 11(3 + 4 + 5) = 11 \times 12 = 132$.

76. Solution: 16.
$a+b+c+d+e+f = 15 \times 6$
$a+b+c+d+e = 15 \times 6 - 10 = 80$.
The answer is 80/5 = 16.

77. Solution: $\dfrac{2}{15}$.

$\dfrac{5x}{2y} = \dfrac{5}{6} \qquad \Rightarrow \qquad 3x = y$.

$\dfrac{2x}{5y} = \dfrac{2x}{5 \times 3x} = \dfrac{2}{15}$.

78. Solution: 76.
$\left\lfloor \dfrac{1000}{13} \right\rfloor = 76$.

79. Solution: 13.
$221 = 13 \times 17$.
$247 = 13 \times 19$.
The answer is 13.

80. Solution: 7.
$\sqrt[3]{49} \times \sqrt[6]{49} = 49^{\frac{1}{3}} \times 49^{\frac{1}{6}} = 49^{\frac{1}{3}+\frac{1}{6}} = 49^{\frac{1}{2}} = 7$.

Made in the USA
Columbia, SC
08 January 2018